What to do . . .

When GOD Doesn't Follow Your Plan

Mark R. Littleton

ACCENT BOOKS
Denver, Colorado

ACCENT BOOKS

A division of Accent Publications, Inc.
12100 West Sixth Avenue
P.O. Box 15337
Denver, Colorado 80215

Copyright © 1989 Mark R. Littleton
Printed in the United States of America

Library of Congress Catalog Card Number 88-83418

ISBN 0-89636-249-3

CONTENTS

To my mother and father,
Richard and Elizabeth Littleton,
who by their example
taught me much about
endurance, determination,
commitment, and love.

INTRODUCTION/
SO MANY DISILLUSIONED DREAMERS

Ever get discouraged? Depressed? Down and troubled and without a helping hand? Feeling like all is lost, the end has come, hope is gone, the devil has won?

We all have. It's usually not so difficult to handle. Often it passes in a day.

But have you ever been disillusioned, terrifically disillusioned—maybe even with God, Jesus, the Bible, Christianity, faith, church, yourself? Have things in life ever reached below bottom?

We have several terms for it.

"Total burnout."

"Totally destroyed."

"A total failure."

Somehow the word "total" epitomizes the feeling. It takes in everything. Like teargas, it billows through our soul with great heaves of hurt. Like a flooded house, the mud goes right up the wallpaper, along the ceiling, and through to the next floor. Like darkness, it hovers over, under, around, and through. Your flashlight's dead. Your nerves are frazzled. And there are strange, hideous noises going on out there in the quiet.

I have seen Christians caught in the bolted and locked cage of disillusionment. There's no joy. No hope. No reason to plod on.

No, they're not suicidal. They're just . . . empty.

For some, it's like a midlife crisis. They feel as though the air's been punched out of them. They lie gasping on the floor, unable to catch a new breath of hope.

For others, it's like a stuck organ note. Every song they play features this one note shrieking in the background. First they try to play around it. Then they try to include it. Then, they simply try to tolerate it. But it soon reaches a point of painful pitch. Everything in the song cries, "You are nothing. Your plans are nothing. God doesn't care about you. You don't count."

The Christian is not immune. You can get out there ten, twenty years down faith's highway and take a hard look back. You may see only remnants of your work. A disciple here. A drop-out there. A class or two that succeeded. Forlorn attempts at witnessing. Scriptures memorized, now forgotten. Great plans to read through the Bible in a year, never achieved.

Oh, the dreams we have! Writing that bestseller. Winning the Nobel Prize. Becoming a senator. Finding a cure for cancer. Having the biggest Bible class in the city. Leading scores to Christ.

Too many Christians who began on fire end in flames. People who gave themselves without stint to the Lord and His kingdom suddenly make an abrupt turnaround.

One man I know went through a bitter period of illness. Daily he questioned, "Why did God let this happen to me?" But eventually, his answer became, "God didn't let this happen to me; there is no God."

So many people are disillusioned.

- The garage mechanic who accepted Christ and expected his family to follow, but they haven't. His wife remains an unbeliever. His children ridicule his beliefs.

- The husband now separated from his wife—he went to counseling. He tried to apply Scripture to his problems. But his wife doesn't want him anymore.

- The teenager who determines to follow God's Word and not date non-Christians has no dates at all. Now.

- The pastor who went to the conference at the huge church in California learned all the key principles. He began applying them. But nothing is happening. This, for three years now.

- The businessman who refused to lie to make a sale.

He can't seem to make his quota. His boss told him last week that if he doesn't make it this year, he's out.

Disillusionment may be one of Satan's best and mightiest weapons against those who seek to live by faith.

I once read a story about all of hell gathering to develop a worldwide strategy. Various devils offered their ideas about how to wreck the Christian's walk with the Lord. One suggested, "I will get him to commit gross sin." That was a good idea, but not always practical, and not universal.

Another suggested, "I will tell him all his ideas about God are wrong. That God doesn't really love him. That God never cared to begin with."

"Too straightforward," answered Satan. "He'll never accept it."

Then one younger devil suggested, "I have it! I'll disillusion his soul."

"How?" asked Satan.

"I'll give him false expectations about God, the kingdom, and the faith. Tell him God will never allow bad things to come into his life. Tell him he'll go far, be wealthy, do wonders for Christ. Every day, those expectations will slam against reality and the world we control. At last he'll become disillusioned and give up."

Moments later, all of hell was shrieking with glee. They had the universal weapon.

A Definition

What is disillusionment? Dictionaries define it as being relieved or deprived of illusion.

That leads to a second question: What is an "illusion"? *Webster's New Collegiate Dictionary* defines it as "the state or fact of being intellectually deceived or misled; a misleading image presented to the vision."

To be disillusioned is the bitter disappointment that comes at learning certain hopes or dreams will never become reality.

For instance, one day I walked into our bookroom at Seminary and saw a student sitting at a table behind a stack of books. He was selling his library because his wife didn't want to go into fulltime ministry. He said, with tears in his eyes, "It became such a battle, I had to make a decision. This is it."

For the Christian to become disillusioned with God or his faith means discovering that certain things you thought were true have turned out to be untrue.

Suppose a Christian reads Jeremiah 29:11-12 and comes away believing that God has a plan for his life that excludes all problems, trials, and calamities, what will happen when a severe trial strikes? Disillusionment. He's disappointed, grieved that, seemingly, God's promise didn't turn out to be true. In actuality, though, what was untrue was the believer's interpretation of God's promise. Nonetheless, it can cause incredible emotional and mental pain.

How It Happens

How does one become disillusioned in the Christian life?

Usually slowly and subtly. First, an idea takes root. Maybe that God promises to do this certain thing in your life—make it a success, bring you a mate, win you an award. Or perhaps it's a Scripture you think you understand and are applying. God is supposed to do this if you do that. Or, maybe it's the fact that the Lord has allowed you to do something you bitterly regret. A mistake. A sin. A wound. It could be anything. But once the idea is fixed in place, then Satan makes his play. When God doesn't come through the way you thought He should, Satan steps in. That mate doesn't come along. Success eludes you. The sin nags away, and you still feel tremendous guilt, no release. Satan whispers, "Okay, explain that one. Either God's being tough, He doesn't know what He's doing, or He's a liar—which is more probable." Or, "See God really doesn't care about you."

Now you begin to doubt God. Neither He, Christianity, or your relationship with Him is turning out the way you thought it would. A growing sense of disillusionment and discouragement sets in. Gradually, all the lessons and habits you so diligently cultivated—Bible study, memorization of the Word, prayer, church-going, witnessing, application of Scripture to problems—slide away. Soon it dawns on you that there are no distinctives left in your life to make you different from the rest of the world.

It Can Go Up

Disillusionment doesn't always lead down, though. Sometimes—even frequently—it leads up. It can drive you into the arms of Jesus so that you learn the truth and become disillusionment-proof. Truth always erases illusions.

If you have ever reached the end of the Christian rainbow and found nothing but week-old mayonnaise on rye, you're a prime candidate for Satan's grand disillusion. On the other hand, you may be on the brink of some of life's greatest adventures.

More importantly, you're in good company. The Bible features a number of disillusioned believers. Saints who reached for the sky and came down face forward into the dirt. But God didn't leave them there. He never leaves any of His beloved. "Those whom I love, I reprove and discipline." He said in Revelation 3:19. And, "He who began a good work in you will perfect it until the day of Christ Jesus" (Philippians 1:6). James 2:1 warns us, "My brethren, do not hold your faith in our glorious Lord Jesus Christ with an attitude of personal favoritism."

It's not the uplook that counts, or the downlook; it's the outlook—the attitude. The worst thing about disillusionment is that it makes you think it's no use having dreams and hopes as a Christian. They'll never come true, so why even try? But I'm convinced God *does* want us to dream—big dreams—and to think far beyond the norms of this world.

This book will look at a number of people who experienced disillusionment and develop some principles about how they overcame it. More importantly, we'll look at the bedrock principles that every Christian must develop in order to become disillusionment-proof. It centers around our realization of God's sovereignty and our acceptance and understanding of God's will.

Disillusionment is no fun, and it provides no reason to wake up in the morning. But no one has to live that way. I hope this book will become part of the answer for you.

PART I: CASES

*A look at five biblical characters who experienced
disillusionment and what they did about it.*

1/THAT QUESTION GOD SO RARELY ANSWERS

I had only recently become a Christian. A close friend didn't like my new outlook, though, and told me so. I tried to explain my new hopes and ideas. But he dismissed it all as nonsense. Then he turned me to the subject of evil.

"You know, several years ago I went to a funeral at one of those conservative churches you go to now. It was for a child who had died a horrid death from leukemia. Everyone knew the child would die. But it was the pastor's message at the funeral that enraged us. Do you know what he told us?"

He didn't wait for me to answer.

"He said that though we might not understand why this child was taken, God was still wise and had a good reason for taking him. Can you imagine that?"

My friend looked at me with angry, skeptical eyes.

I tried to stammer out a reply. But he went on.

"It was the coldest, most callous answer I'd ever heard. I'll never set foot in that church. In fact, that family who lost the child was horrified, too. It was so insensitive. The wisdom of God! A 'good reason' for taking him. Come on. And you're trying to tell me that you're into this same religion? Grow up."

I felt as though the wind had been knocked out of me. What could I say? What could anyone say? Leukemia. A seven-year-old boy.

"God is wise."

"God is good."

It seems to make little sense.

Unexplained Tragedy

Unexplained tragedies provoke some of the worst forms of doubt for Christians. We ask, "Why?" and the heavens remain silent, seemingly uncaring. We cry out, "How could you let this happen?" and God seems to disappear into the roofwork. It's one question God rarely answers directly even though we often try to answer it for Him.

We certainly don't plan on these things happening.

What do we plan on? Oh, you know, happiness, joy, fun, peace, fulfillment—things like that. Not suffering, pain, agony, and destruction.

But God also has a plan. Sometimes that plan brings stark and unexplainable tragedy into our lives that not only takes our breath away, but also rocks our faith, our hope, our confidence.

Is there help for such situations?

Unequalled Tragedy

One of God's answers for us is the book of Job. His story is one of unequalled tragedy in human history. God asked Satan if he'd noticed this faithful man, Job. Satan had, but replied the only reason Job was faithful was because God had given him so much. So God put Job into Satan's hands. He allowed Satan to attack his possessions and family. Job lost everything. But he didn't deny God.

After that, God and Satan had another confrontation. God brought up the fact that Job hadn't cursed Him even though Satan had said he would. Satan replied, "Skin for skin! . . . Put forth Thy hand now, and touch his bone and his flesh; he will curse Thee to Thy face" (Job 2:4-5).

Again, God let Satan attack. This time Satan destroyed Job's health. He was smitten with running boils from head to foot. It might have been a form of elephantiasis, leprosy, or skin cancer. Whatever it was, it tore Job's soul.

Nonetheless, Job never cursed God.

But he did begin to question. "Why? What did I do? Why me?"

He became disillusioned, wondering if God was unjust and uncaring.

Wanting An Explanation

What disillusions us in these circumstances is that God usually doesn't offer us reasons why such things happen. He simply tells us to keep on believing, keep on being faithful.

But how? How can you keep on believing when . . .

　. . . a child is born with spina bifida?

　. . . a husband loses a job just when it seemed the door had cracked open on real opportunity?

　. . . a respected leader commits adultery, and then tries to hide it?

　. . . your church suffers from disunity and seems headed for a split?

　. . . your family goes bankrupt?

　. . . your home burns down (or you're robbed, etc.)?

Add your own disasters to the list. The questions remain, stark and vivid. How can I just accept it and believe anyway?

I recall the day my grandfather suffered a stroke, was placed in a nursing home for recovery, and my grandparents' home of over fifty years had to be sold. It was a wrenching decision for my parents. But my grandmother's own cry is what has always stuck with me. I was a new Christian at the time. I stayed with her overnight to help her get through. I awakened at two a.m. and heard her muffled sobbing in the next room. After several minutes of debate, I went in and said, "Grandmom, what's wrong?"

She said, "Everything's gone wrong, honey. It's all over for us. Grandpop will never get well."

I tried to encourage her.

But she put her face in her handkerchief and wept, saying, "I just don't understand what God is doing anymore."

Who was I to explain? Even if I could?

When tragedy does crash into our lives, one of our first reactions is to ask, "Why? Why me? Why this? Why now?" We suppose that if we only knew the answer, if God explained it all, then everything would make sense, we could accept it and go on.

But is that true? Would God's explanation satisfy? Would that make it all right?

The Cry for an Explanation

That was precisely what Job wanted to know: *why?* Look at him in several passages. He demands in chapter 6, verse 24, "Teach me, and I will be silent; and show me how I have erred." In 10:2, he laments, "I will say to God, 'Do not condemn me; let me know why Thou dost contend with me.' " In 13:3 he says, "I would speak to the Almighty, and I desire to argue with God." In 13:22-23 again he cries, "Call, and I will answer; or let me speak, then reply to me. How many are my iniquities and sins? Make known to me my rebellion and my sin." On and on throughout Job's speeches he challenges God. "Let's take this into court. Let's discuss it. Just tell me why, then I'll be content."

More Questions Than Answers!

But would that be enough? In Job's case, had he learned that the reason he was suffering was because God gave Satan an opportunity to destroy him, he might easily have become far more upset than he already was.

Chapters 1 and 2 of Job can baffle us. If God told you the reason for your tragedy was because Satan had challenged Him to a duel and you got caught in the middle, wouldn't you be just a little outraged?

Could God Explain?

More importantly, could we understand God's explanation of our tragedy even if He did explain?

Consider several problems.

First, *God's working on an infinite scale; we're finite.* For God to explain Job's tragedy, He'd have to start with Lucifer's rebellion in heaven. Then He'd have to move through all the events in history up to Job's situation. Such an explanation would take volumes and volumes, whole libraries of facts. Is that the kind of explanation we'd want? No. But what kind could God give? The only kind that ultimately would be acceptable would be one in which God showed us His perfect wisdom. And such an explanation would require an analysis of all recorded and unrecorded history!

Imagine trying to explain to your pet dog Joshua why he has to have rabies shots. Is it possible? Never in a million dog lives. Joshua just doesn't have the mental equipment to comprehend.

The problem is that God cannot simplify His explanations sufficiently to satisfy us. His ways of reasoning and thinking are not like ours. He has all the facts at His disposal. He knows every detail of a situation. Moreover, He has perfect wisdom. How could He convey all of this in one simple answer? It's impossible for finite minds to comprehend that perfect wisdom.

There's another problem: *we have a fallen nature.* Even though we're new creatures in Christ, we constantly wrestle with the problems of depravity and fallenness. It intrudes at every point. Corruption taints every thought of our hearts (Romans 3:10,23; 8:5-8; Jeremiah 17:9). It's only as we lean on Scripture, let His Word color our thinking, that we come into harmony with God. But our fallenness will naturally fight against any explanation He offers (I Corinthians 1:25).

The third problem with an explanation from God is this: *He's already given us one, and we don't pay attention to it!* Everyone of us probably has his own Bible, if not several. We have it in several different translations, with side notes, cross references, commentaries, and every other help conceived by man. But what do we do with those Bibles? Often, everything but read them, memorize them, and meditate on them.

I was horrified to learn some years ago about a talk show on television involving homosexuals and Christians. The homosexuals maintained the Bible was on their side and said nothing against their chosen sexual orientation. The Christians disagreed. An argument crackled back and forth. Suddenly, the commentator stopped everything and said to the homosexual group, "You say the Bible supports your position. You show me where." He turned to the Christians and stated the same thing. Then everyone went to work.

The gay faction read off a few words that had nothing to do with the problem. Then it was the Christians' turn. Do you know that in an audience of some 300 people, not one Christian could cite a specific statement of God on the subject?

That's stupefying. No, more than that. It's unnerving, appalling, even mortifying.

Yet, it underlines a truth. God *has* given us explanations on every subject. It's called the Bible. Yet, we repeatedly accuse

Him of being silent, uncaring, disinterested, and unloving when we suffer personal difficulties.

Clearly, our problem is not with God. It's with our own laziness. We simply don't know enough of the Word to apply it to our needs.

God's Kind of Explanation

Just the same, God did give Job an explanation—of sorts. What He didn't do was tell Job specifically why his tragedies happened to him. But He did something else, something that was ultimately far more valuable.

First, He set things in context. When God spoke from the whirlwind, He asked Job a series of questions even scientists today can't answer.

Where were you when I laid the foundation of the earth (38:4)?
How did I make it stay in place (38:6)?
How did I keep the sea from spilling out into the air (38:8-11)?
Can you make the earth rotate and keep the morning in its place (38:12)?
What keeps the sea full all the time (38:16)?
What causes snow? Why does water expand instead of contract when it freezes? (38:22f)?
What keeps the stars in place (38:31-33)?

What was God doing? Humiliating Job?

No. Job had challenged God's wisdom, asking how He could allow the disasters to strike. Now God needed to set His wisdom in context. It was a little exam. "All right, Job, since you're questioning how I run the universe, let me ask you a few simple questions."

God was not putting Job down. He was being a firm, loving parent. If we're going to accuse God of being unwise in His administration, we'd better be prepared to back it up by showing how much wiser we are.

God set His wisdom and power in perspective for Job. He ends with the words, "Will the faultfinder contend with the

Almighty? Let him who reproves God answer it" (Job 40:2).

Second, God created a situation which readied Job for the truth. By raising these questions and facing him with such devastating problems, God created new humility in Job. He became ready to accept things on God's terms.

Heretofore he'd been demanding all sorts of things of God. "I will give full vent to my complaint . . . . Let me know why Thou dost contend with me . . . . According to Thy knowledge I am indeed not guilty; Yet there is no deliverance from Thy hand" (Job 10:1-7). It was arrogant. Perhaps understandable arrogance, considering what Job had been through, but something that had to be dealt with.

What happens in such a situation? Blindness. You can't see the truth because Satan obscures it. "The god of this world has blinded the minds of the unbelieving," said Paul (II Corinthians 4:4). God strips away such blindness by bringing us to our knees, to repentance.

That's precisely where He took Job. In Job 40:4-5 Job says, "Behold, I am insignificant; what can I reply to Thee? I lay my hand on my mouth. Once I have spoken, and I will not answer; even twice, and I will add no more."

Job recognized his insignificance. He saw God's greatness and the power of His wisdom. But there was still another problem.

Third, God led him to see his sin. He'd dealt somewhat with Job's pride. But more excavation work had to be done. Job needed to see that God had a right to do as He wanted. That God was sovereign. That as His subject, Job owed Him absolute—even unquestioning—obedience.

Thus, God raised more impossible questions.

"Can you annul My judgment" (40:8)?

"Will you condemn Me that you may be justified" (40:8)?

"Do you have power like Me?" (40:9)?

God goes on with more questions. But the end result is found in Job's words.

"I know that Thou canst do all things, and that no purpose of Thine can be thwarted" (42:2). He recognized God's sovereignty and right to run the universe as He pleased.

Quoting God (Job 38:2), Job recognizes the truth of God's words. Who was he, a creature, to tell the Creator how to govern, when he didn't even know the most basic elements of governing?

"Therefore I have declared that which I did not understand, things too wonderful for me, which I did not know" (42:3). In other words, "I didn't know what I was talking about."

"Hear, now, and I will speak; I will ask you and you instruct me" (42:4). "Therefore I retract, And I repent in dust and ashes" (42:6). In other words, "I'm ready to listen now, Lord."

Job was not only brought to his knees, God took up residence in his mind and heart. Job had seen God and he now knew the truth. It would affect him forever.

A teacher I know used to tell his students: "When we ask God hard questions, He doesn't always give us answers. Rather, He gives us Himself."

That's what Job came away with as a result of his disillusionment. He had a greater vision of God. He knew God personally. He could worship now—not just as part of a routine—but with abandon, with joy, with genuine love, with all his heart, soul, mind, and might.

An Imagined Conversation

Suppose in an imagined conversation with God, we said:

"Why did this happen, Lord?"

God answers, "Mark (Mary, Tom), do you believe I love you?"

"Yes."

"Do you believe I'm perfectly wise, know all things, and am running the universe according to perfect wisdom?"

You answer confidently, "Yes."

"Do you believe I'm in total charge of all things, the Sovereign of the universe, and that nothing could happen unless I, in My wisdom, allowed it?"

You hesitate a moment, but nod your head. "Yes."

"Do you believe that ultimately My thoughts are not your thoughts and that the reason I do things may not always make sense to you?"

You glance down at your feet, pause a moment, and think about that one. Then you say, "Yes."

"And, do you believe that I am far greater than you in knowledge and power and that any explanation I give would literally fill a volume the size of the entire *Encyclopedia Brittanica* in order for you to even come close to understanding the answer?"

You look up a moment and for the first time are astounded at the majesty and greatness of God. You bow your head. "Yes, Lord, I believe you are this way."

"Then there's only one thing left for you to do."

"What's that?"

"Cease demanding explanations, and trust Me, because I am worthy of your trust and believe that there are good reasons for these things, even though I may not explain them to you."

Suddenly you see that that is, indeed, the answer. You bow in worship. "I trust you, Lord, even though I don't always understand."

A close friend of mine was going through a divorce. Her husband of ten years simply didn't want her any more. It was, for her, a wretched, soul-tearing experience.

One day we sat down to talk about it. She told me through her tears, "You know, I don't understand any of this, Mark. But

I've come to treasure the words of Job, 'Though He slay me, I will hope in Him' (13:15). That's all I really have—faith in the Lord. I know He has it all in hand even though I can't see it. So I've determined to trust Him. No matter what."

I came away marveling. And with renewed faith in facing my own trials.

2/A BIG DREAM GOES BUST

The very first words of the first chapter of the world's most popular book on positive thinking say this:

"Believe in yourself! Have faith in your abilities! Without a humble but reasonable confidence in your own powers you cannot be successful or happy. But with sound self-confidence you can succeed." [1]

Oh?

Multitudes of books exhort us to realize that we can capture any dream, achieve any achievement, accomplish any goal—if we'll just dare to try. "If you think you can, you can," is the catch phrase.

For some it becomes a virtual mantra that they repeat morning, noon, and night. I remember attending a "positive thinking rally" many years ago. One speaker exhorted us to get up in the morning, look ourselves in the mirror, and say with utmost fervor, "I can do it. I can accomplish all I desire. My dreams are in reach." Another informed us, "Just remove negative thoughts from your mind, and you can go anywhere, do anything. It's all in the power of the mind."

Disillusionment Through Thinking Big

Nonetheless, disabling disillusionment can destroy people whose big thinking turns bad. Richard Nixon found that out with Watergate. Ivan Boesky discovered it on Wall Street in the 1987 insider trading scandal. If we put together some gigantic plan for success and God has another plan altogether, we enter a conflict that can lead literally to our demise.

The Biblical Example

The worst case on record that I know of happened to Elijah, one of the greatest, miracle-wielding prophets of the Old Testament. We find him in I Kings 18 at the head of a one man crusade to reform the nation of Israel. His God-given means to accomplish that end is a rather remarkable one: by stopping all rainfall in the land.

King Ahab responded to Elijah's drought by going on a search and destroy mission for the prophet. But after three and a half years of rainlessness, Elijah came out of hiding. He met the king and issued a stark challenge: "Now then send and gather to me all Israel at Mount Carmel, together with 450 prophets of Baal and 400 prophets of the Asherah, who eat at Jezebel's table" (I Kings 18:19). He had provoked the ultimate showdown. The theological fight at the Mt. Carmel corral. Elijah—with God—planned to take them all on.

Elijah challenged those 950 prophets to a duel that would decide whose was the true God. The specifics were these: each side would build an altar. They would then prepare an ox for a burnt offering, with all the wood and implements necessary. However, they were not to fire it up. They were each to call on the name of their god (Baal was their god of fire), and the god which answered by sending fire from heaven was the true God.

Rather risky business. But Elijah had tremendous confidence. He thought wondrously big, and he knew his God would act.

Meanwhile, the 950 prophets prepared their sacrifice and began calling on their god. When nothing happened, Elijah began to taunt them with sarcasm and jokes. "You'd better call louder, boys. He might be occupied with other business, or maybe he's gone on a vacation. Of course, he may just be asleep, so try to wake him up" (I Kings 18:27).

The prophets answered with louder calls to Baal. They even

began cutting themselves with swords and lances. This was customary in pagan rituals in order to win the attention of their god with their ardor. It was a sign of conviction, determination, and repentance. As they cut themselves, they confessed their sins. It also lent itself to inducing an ecstatic frenzy, which was considered a part of their worship. The pain, loss of blood, and resultant lightheadedness often produced hallucinations and strange, crazed behavior that onlookers called "ecstasy," supposedly caused by the power of the god. They did this from morning until evening.

Nonetheless, their efforts came to nothing. No voice spoke. No fire ignited. The people themselves even became bored.

At that point, Elijah called everyone to his side of the mountain. It's possible he had chosen Mt. Carmel because it was a worship site for the people of Israel after the kingdom had split, and they no longer had their own temple. The altar of the Lord had been torn down, possibly during Ahab's reign when he tried to eliminate Jehovah worship from Israel.

Elijah rebuilt that altar. He carried in twelve stones—one for each tribe of Israel—then dug a trench around it. He arranged a pyre of wood and placed the sacrificial pieces of the ox on top. Then he sent some of the young men to bring four large pitchers, over a gallon each, from a local spring. They poured the water on the ox meat and the wood. It overflowed into the trench. He repeated this action two more times.

Elijah then called on God.

> "O Lord, the God of Abraham, Isaac and Israel, today let it be known that Thou art God in Israel, and that I am Thy servant, and that I have done all these things at Thy word. Answer me, O Lord, answer me, that this people may know that Thou, O Lord, art God, and that Thou hast turned their heart back

again" (I Kings 18:36-37).

BAM!

No knife cuts. No calls. No loud crying. Just like that, God answered. Fire from heaven consumed everything—the sacrifice, the wood, the stones, and the water. Nothing but a huge burned circle was left on the ground.

What happened then?

Everyone fell on their faces screaming, "The Lord, He is God; the Lord, He is God."

Elijah moved quickly. "Seize the prophets of Baal!"

The people jumped up, grabbed all 950 of them, and took them down to the brook Kishon. There Elijah, and possibly others, slew every one of them.

In an hour, Baal worship was ended in Israel. Undoubtedly King Ahab watched, probably both fascinated and aghast. Perhaps he was thinking, "What on earth will I tell Jezebel?"

Elijah immediately told Ahab to eat and drink because a huge shower was sweeping in from the sea. Then Elijah went up to the top of Mt. Carmel again, crouched down, put his face between his knees, and prayed. Seven times he sent his servant to look. On the seventh time, the servant saw a small cloud. In a few minutes it became a thunderhead. Then the sky grew black, the rain descended, and for the first time in three and a half years, Israelite soil drank water.

The Revival of 860 B.C.

The moment Ahab saw the rain, he bounded into his chariot and raced to Jezreel, the site of the king's palace. Elijah, however, received supernatural strength from God to run ahead of Ahab. He ran to Jezreel and arrived before Ahab.

I'm convinced Elijah expected to witness the beginning of a great revival after the confrontation on Mt. Carmel. The whole purpose of the confrontation was to prove that God was God, ruler of Israel as much as Judah, and that Baal was an impotent idol. I'm sure he figured that once God revealed Himself that way, Ahab and all of Israel would repent.

During his years in hiding and exile, Elijah had believed in God and carried out His incredible plan for revival. Everything happened the way God said it would. The rain stopped. God exposed the truth on Mt. Carmel. Israel came to their knees in fear. And now the revival could begin. Elijah was thinking as big as anyone in history. He saw the whole nation repenting and turning to God in fullness of commitment and worship. It would be the greatest national transformation ever seen.

But something happened.

King Ahab stalked into his palace and informed Jezebel what had happened: God exalted; Baal humiliated; 950 prophets dead.

Did Jezebel fall to her knees, crying, "The Lord, He is God"? No. Instead, the vengeful mistress of Israel issued an ultimatum to Elijah: "So may the gods do to me and even more, if I do not make your life as the life of one of them by tomorrow about this time" (I Kings 19:2).

As the messenger stood before Elijah delivering Jezebel's death threat, you'd think Elijah would only laugh. "I'll let God handle her!" At the very least he could have said, "Believe me, if I can kill off 950 prophets I can certainly deal with one irate woman!"

But that's not what he did.

Stark Raving Terror

First Kings 19:3 says, "He was afraid and arose and ran for his life and came to Beersheba, which belongs to Judah, and left his servant there." In other words, Elijah headed for the hills! Beersheba was located on the southern edge of Judah, at least 90 miles south of Jezreel! And that was just his first stop. This was one frightened prophet!

How could all this happen? In a word, disillusionment. Elijah had expected a massive turn to God from the Mt. Carmel demonstration. But what did he get? A threat on his life, not a single soul saved, and a new manhunt after him.

He sat down under a juniper tree in the desert and asked that God let him die. Things were so bad, so hopeless, Elijah saw no way out.

Several years ago, while serving as a pastor, I began thinking big. My church had about fifty regulars, and I wanted to turn them into master evangelists and disciplers. I worked it all out on paper. If I discipled someone for six months, turned him into a first-rate servant of Jesus and sent him out to disciple someone else the next six months, I calculated that at such a rate of multiplication— with each of us discipling someone new every six months— we'd have 25,000 disciples in ten years. I was excited. I made up a memo, passed it out to everyone, then cranked up the spiritual rotors and preached a great sermon about commitment. We decided to meet every weekday morning at 6:30 A.M. before work. I'd teach the people how to study Scripture, memorize verses, and develop a potent prayer life.

What happened?

The first Monday twenty-five people showed up. I was in glory. We studied like we'd never studied. We prayed like we'd never prayed. We memorized, fellowshiped, and waited on God. This was the beginning of the revival of Maryland, perhaps even the whole U.S.A. Perhaps even the whole world. It was all starting in our little church in Glen Burnie, Maryland.

Well, that first week was incredible. Everyone coming. Everyone excited.

But then the grind set in. The second week the numbers dwindled.

In five weeks, I had about three people meeting sporadically. I went into my office, sat down, and looked at the ceiling. "What happened, Lord?"

It was as though He spoke inside my heart. There were two statements. "Mark, you forgot two things: people's hearts— and Me."

Oh. Just that? People's hearts and God?

Right. But that's more than enough.

In a sense, that's what happened to Elijah. He'd forgotten certain things. He forgot to reckon with the problem of the heart and the involvement of God Himself. What would the people do? And what was God's plan? In other words, in the midst of *his* awesome plans, he forgot to consult the God of the overall PLAN.

Thinking big can be thinking bad if what you're thinking depends on people and doesn't include the clear involvement of the Lord.

Why and How?

How had Elijah gotten into this fix?

Let me offer three factors that may have contributed to his situation.

First, he wielded incredible spiritual power. He stopped the rain. God hid him perfectly and fed him miraculously by the brook. Later, he watched the Lord provide food for the widow. He raised her son from the dead. That's a kind of power no one had seen in Hebrew history since the time of Moses. And Moses was Israel's greatest leader and prophet.

That kind of power can make you forget something important: people. You get so wrapped up in what you want to see happen, that you forget the people to whom you want it to happen. You become de-personalized.

I'm not sure this happened to Elijah. But it may have had a part in it.

Second, Elijah spent much time alone. Coupled with his surging power in the hand of God was the fact that Elijah was isolated, alone, with no other person whom he could use as a sounding board for his ideas. Loners are often great leaders. But there is wisdom in many counselors (Proverbs 11:14). Perhaps he let his head get ahead of reality. He failed to see all the possibilities that could result from his actions. His expectations, while they soared, also put him on schedule for a big letdown. Much like Peter, Elijah took his eyes off the Lord and let fear overcome him.

Third, Elijah possessed a towering commitment to the Lord. Christians who are that committed to the Lord often fail to understand people who are not.

I remember a professor in seminary railing at us in one of his classes. He said, "Sometimes I feel like walking into that chapel and saying, 'Everyone who wants to go for broke and give it all to God, stand up over here. And everyone who doesn't want to, leave. Make room for somebody who does want to give it all to God.'"

Those words smacked of power. I loved them. But our prof didn't leave us there. He added, "Gentlemen, I'd like to do that. But I can't. Because God's not working the same way in everyone. Some of those guys out there need some time before they're gung ho. And I have to give them that time. I can't stymie God's Word just because I'd like some more committed bodies in my classes."

That hit me.

I tend to think that was part of Elijah's problem. He thought in black and white terms. "It's either this or that, boys. No in-betweens. Now let's get on with it." He couldn't see people in flux, in the process of transformation.

What To Do Now?

So we arrive at the classic question: "Whaddaya do now?"

Elijah's so disillusioned and discouraged out there in Beersheba that he's ready to die. He's frightened, hungry, upset, depressed, down and out for the count. What would God do to help His prophet?

Physical sustenance. The first thing that had to be done was to get Elijah back in good physical condition. He'd just traveled ninety miles in an all-out panic. So God let him sleep. After a long rest, God sent an angel to feed him "bread cake baked on hot stones" and "a jar of water" (19:6).

Notice God didn't give him a lecture at this point. He didn't drill home a verse of Scripture, didn't slap him on the back, and say, "Come on, let's get going, prophet. We've got work to do." No, He let him sleep, eat, and sleep some more. Good therapy. Sometimes, when you're discouraged, it's the simple things you need more than any spiritual anodyne.

After his second sleep, the angel gave him a second meal. So great was this gift of food and sleep that Elijah finally arose and went "in the strength of that food forty days and forty nights to Horeb, the mountain of God" (19:8).

Time to think. Mt. Horeb is located in the southern region of the Sinai peninsula, approximately 170 miles south of Beersheba. Again, what God did was critical to helping the prophet through his disillusionment. God gave him time to think, to review, to relive a few scenes, and wonder. Elijah may even have taken a meandering, roundabout way to Horeb, perhaps simply wandering, meditating, arguing, praying, thinking.

It's obvious that Elijah was still distressed. As soon as he arrived at Horeb, he hid in a cave.

An object lesson. Still, up to this point, apparently God had not spoken to Elijah. He had renewed him physically, given him time to think and talk out some of his feelings, but now God challenged him.

"What are you doing here, Elijah?" (19:9).

Elijah replied, "I have been very zealous for the Lord, the God of hosts; for the sons of Israel have forsaken Thy covenant, torn down Thine altars and killed Thy prophets with the sword. And I alone am left; and they seek my life, to take it away" (I Kings 19:10).

God didn't argue. He gave Elijah an object lesson.

First, He spun a windstorm. Rocks tore out and split in the wind. Trees were blown down. But Elijah just tightened his cape around him. He knew that this was God's power, but not God's passing.

Second, there was an earthquake. Underneath his feet, the ground slid. But it passed. Again, he realized God wasn't in the earthquake. It was just a display.

Then, flames burst out of the air. A tower of flames, perhaps like the pillar of fire in Moses' day. The heat may have singed Elijah's beard, but God still had not appeared.

Last, there was a "sound of a gentle blowing." It was different. Elijah heard a difference in this sound. He covered his face in his robe, went out, and stood in the entrance to the cave.

Reassurance. Then God spoke again. "What are you doing here, Elijah" (19:13)?

Elijah replied with the same words as earlier, an exact quote.

Again, God didn't argue. He simply gave Elijah a series of tasks—to anoint Hazael as king over Syria; to anoint Jehu as king over Israel; and to appoint Elisha as prophet in his place.

Above all, God told Elijah that there were 7,000 others in Israel who remained loyal to Him. Elijah wasn't alone. He was only one of thousands.

Elijah went from there and found Elisha. We're never told if he anointed the other two men as kings, but we don't need to know. He'd been through a lot. We do know that Elisha became Elijah's companion, ministering to him.

Is Thinking Big Bad?

So we come to the question: Is it bad to think big? Is it bad to concoct gigantic ambitions and plans for God's kingdom?

If we think in terms of what the world tells us—to think big in order to gain the riches, honor, and glory we long for—it is unequivocably bad. It's nothing more than an appeal to man's innate sin, pride. It only increases our problem with ego, self, and selfishness.

On the other hand, God wants us to think His thoughts, and those thoughts are big (Philippians 4:8; Amos 4:13). What does God think in terms of? Eternity. The whole of creation. Galaxies. Light years. God has big ideas about things.

The important issue for us and others like Elijah is this: are we thinking *with* God or *apart from* God? If apart from God, we're in quicksand. But if we're thinking with Him, we're on rock as solid as earth itself.

FOOTNOTES

[1] Norman V. Peale, *The Power of Positive Thinking,* (Greenwich, CT: Fawcett Publications, 1952), p. 13.

3/A Total Loss

He was, as they say in contemporary lingo, my "main man." I called him, "Grandpop."

His impact on my life was a succession of firsts.

One of my first memories of him was at Christmas when I was five. I received a little coin bank. He produced a quarter from his pocket and held it up. "See this," he said. "I'll be the first one to put something in your bank." A quarter could buy a lot back then. I watched him drop it in the slot, a little miffed that he hadn't simply given me the money for myself. But he noticed my chagrin. He looked at me, and said, "Now, do you want to know how to get it out?"

Did I ever! He told me to get a dinner knife from the kitchen.

My mother remarked, "Dad, you shouldn't show him that."

He showed me anyway. Then told me to do it only in an emergency.

He gave me my first jackknife. He taught me how to throw it so it stuck.

He taught me how to split logs for firewood. He'd hold the wedge in place, then tell me to sock it with the sledgehammer. "But I might hit your hand," I'd wail in fear. He'd reply, "What kind of dumb bunny do you think I am? Now sock it!"

At the last microsecond he'd let go and the log would split cleanly.

When he retired, he bought the family's first house trailer and took off west with Grandmom. The next summer, they took me. Yellowstone Park. The Rockies. Wyoming. Montana. We saw it all. Caught more fish than we could eat. I froze several and brought them home for the others who hadn't had a chance to go.

I thought he would live forever. Then, when I was fourteen, he had a stroke. It crippled him. He couldn't speak, couldn't walk. I didn't know what to say. Somehow I knew his pain was even greater than mine. He had to sit in his wheelchair watching us swim and water ski. He couldn't even raise his arm and shout, "Go!"

I tried to understand what had happened, to believe that things would get better, that soon he'd be out feeding the chipmunks, splitting firewood, and working at his workbench.

But it wasn't to be. A few weeks after the first stroke, he suffered another massive stroke. Late that night, after I'd gone to bed, Dad woke me. He said, "Grandpop died tonight."

I put my head into my pillow and pretended to go back to sleep. Dad said nothing more.

At the funeral, I told myself I wouldn't cry.

But I did. I couldn't stop. Every time the feeling would come on, I'd duck into a bathroom or go to another room. I didn't understand it, this sense of loss, of hopelessness. At the time, I wasn't a Christian, and for me, this was the end.

Even now as I write, I find myself fighting the tears. I don't even know what it was that he had. Maybe, just that he loved me. And I knew it.

A loss, especially of an intimate friend, can fell you. It can lead to intense grief, depression, anger, and sometimes disillusionment.

Unfortunately, we live in a world shot through with evil, and above all, the evil of death. Since the Garden of Eden, God's plan for every human being has included death. Yet, few of us accept that reality. When we lose a loved one, there's a rage about it, an agony, a despair. Somehow we think it happened too soon. It should have been later, sometime down the road.

For the Christian, death should hold no power against us. We have a risen Savior, one who has conquered death and one who assures us He shall conquer it in us. But that still doesn't make a loss any easier to take.

There's at least one person in Scripture whom I'm convinced experienced intense disillusionment as a result of a loss: Thomas.

The Doubter?

We call him "Doubting Thomas," but that's a misnomer. All the disciples doubted. Thomas simply wasn't there the first time Jesus appeared to them, so his doubting lasted a little longer. Through Thomas we see the mind and soul of a man who thought he had lost everything.

Thomas doesn't receive much press in Scripture, but what he did receive is important. It gives us a little insight into the disillusionment that can come through the loss of a loved one, the loss of a vision, the loss of hope.

Some Background

The first time we see Thomas expressing himself occurs in John 11. Some messengers came to Jesus while He was ministering on the other side of the Jordan to tell him Lazarus was sick. Sickness in those days provoked terror. There were few cures. An illness, which today might be handled with a doctor's prescription, could kill back then. But Jesus waited for two more days.

After the two days passed, Jesus told the disciples they'd be going back to Judea. The disciples balked. They said to Him, "Rabbi, the Jews were just now seeking to stone You; and are You going there again?" (John 10:24—11:8).

Jesus answered their question and told them to go.

It was then that Thomas spoke. He said, "Let us also go, that we may die with Him" (John 11:16). It's a cryptic response, even pessimistic; it does seem in line with our idea of Thomas as the doubting disciple, the complete defeatist. But is that what he meant?

Before answering that, let's look at the second time we see him in John. In John 14, Jesus began the great Olivet discourse. He opened with the words, "I go to prepare a place for you." Immediately, Thomas speaks with a hint of fear and terror in his voice. "Lord, we do not know where You are going; how do we know the way?" (John 14:5). Again, we see this strange anxiety that we see only in Thomas. He was genuinely frightened. Jesus leaving?! Impossible.

The third episode is the famous one where Thomas disappears for several days after the crucifixion while Jesus appears to the remaining disciples. It's in that context that Thomas utters the unforgettable words, "Unless I shall see in His hands the imprint of the nails . . . and put my hand into His side, I will not believe" (John 20:25). Eight days later Jesus walks among them, and Thomas falls at His feet, crying, "My Lord and my God!"

How do we put these three episodes together to round out the man?

Three Distinct Traits

The first trait I see in Thomas is *intense loyalty*. Perhaps more than all the other disciples, Thomas possessed a high and holy loyalty to Jesus. He believed intensely. His whole being was involved in his faith—mind, emotions, and will. He had thought deeply about Jesus and had come to the conclusion that He was, indeed, the Messiah. Following Him was unto death. There was no one else, no one after.

The second trait is *total commitment*. This is similar to loyalty, but different. Thomas seemed to know that his life was Jesus or nothing. He was ready to die with Jesus, not just because of who he believed Jesus was, but because of what Jesus represented. For Thomas, Jesus was THE way, THE truth, and THE life. Nothing else would do for him.

The third characteristic is *a lack of self-confidence.* That may seem surprising, but I see it in all that Thomas says and does. He possessed confidence only as he relied on and was with Jesus. That's part of the reason he went into such despair after the cross. The Source of all meaning and confidence in his life had died.

Add up those three traits and what do you have? I would say this: it defines the kind of person who, if he lost Jesus—the Person on whom his whole life was built—would suffer a deeper and greater shattering than any other.

That is why we see Thomas alone after the crucifixion. It destroyed him. Everything he'd lived for had come to nothing. He'd put all his eggs in one basket, and now they were all smashed. Or so it appeared.

The only way to go in such a circumstance is down. It's more than depression. More than discouragement. It's a total, unequivocal disillusionment. And it's focused right on Jesus Himself. For in Thomas's mind, it was Jesus who had let him down. That is why he said he wouldn't believe unless he saw the nailprints. In order to rekindle the kind of faith he'd had up to the crucifixion, he would need absolute proof. He could never be committed to something he considered a hoax, a lie, or a pretense. His heart had to be in it all the way.

It's a strange thing, but I occasionally suffer from similar kinds of fear. Every now and then Satan hits me with, "What if it's all a lie? What if God really isn't immutable? What if I decided to give up the faith?"

Theologically speaking, I know all those things are utterly untrue and absolutely impossible. But those fears make me realize that apart from Jesus I have no hope whatsoever. If

He's not true, if He's not Lord, there's nothing, no hope, no truth, no surety.

Yet, even more than that is my own realization that Jesus Christ is everything to me. We Christians *have* put all our eggs in one basket. We have staked everything on Him. If He really was just a man, just someone who died on a cross, then we have nothing.

I sense that this was part of what Thomas was feeling after the cross and before the resurrection. There was no reason to live anymore. Why struggle? Why keep fighting?

What God Did

But what did the Lord do with it? Did He leave Thomas this way?

Not at all. And He'll never leave you in this condition if this is the place to which you've come. What, then, is God's answer to this disillusionment?

Notice three ideas from John 20:26-29, the passage in which Thomas encounters the risen Christ.

First, Jesus gave Thomas the proof he needed. When Jesus appeared eight days after Thomas's initial statement of not believing until he'd seen the nailprints in His hands, Christ didn't come with a rebuke, proof texts, or hard eyes. No. He invited Thomas to touch, to see, to feel, to find out and be convinced beyond change. He said, "Reach here your finger, and see My hands; and reach here your hand, and put it into My side" (John 21:27).

I love the Lord's humility. No gloss. No veneer. No dillying around. "Touch Me," He says.

You know, one thing I can never do to people who have questions and fears is to say, "Just believe. Don't worry about all these extraneous things."

Even Jesus didn't come at it like that. If a person needs proof, Jesus doesn't respond, "How dare you? Out of My sight!"

No. He invites us to come. "O taste and see that the Lord is good," the Psalmist proclaimed (Psalm 34:8).

More than this, *Jesus demonstrated real love and compassion toward Thomas.*

There's nothing to dispel the disillusionment that comes through loss like the proof of Jesus' love and care.

During my second year in seminary, I was under a pile of work and felt I could not get above it. Most notably, I had to write a paper on a passage in Ephesians, studying through the Greek text, and doing some major mining to expose the jewels. The problem was, I couldn't seem to find any jewels.

One wintry afternoon I headed for my job full of frustration and discouragement. As I walked, I prayed, "Come on, Lord, what gives? Aren't you going to help?"

The wind was frigid. I pulled my coat about me and ducked down. Suddenly, I ran into a tree branch. The whole tree heaved and pitched in the wind. I looked up, a little angry, and noticed a bird's nest on one of the lower braches. I thought at any moment it would catapult off and crash to the ground.

I looked closer. There was a bird in the nest! A little robin. It looked like it was sitting on some eggs.

I moved a little closer, intrigued, forgetting the cold.

The branch whipped up and down, but the bird seemed unmoved. In fact, its eyes were tightly closed. Its head feathers parted in the wind.

The scene was so incredible, I began laughing. A robin was sitting on eggs in a nest that any moment might flip off and slam onto the sidewalk. But that crazy bird! It was unmoved, unworried, fearless. I couldn't help but think of Jesus' words, "Are not two sparrows sold for a cent? And yet not one of them will fall to the ground apart from your Father" (Matthew 10:29). I asked myself, "So what are you so upset about, Littleton?"

It was like a little personal object lesson from the Lord. I felt He was telling me, "I care, Mark. I know what I'm doing. Hang tough. Like the little bird."

Thomas got the same message. He couldn't help himself. He fell at Jesus' feet, exclaiming, "My Lord and my God."

In fact, this may be one of the best texts of the proof of Jesus' deity. Here was a man, totally disillusioned, totally unbelieving, and demanding the most rigorous sorts of proof. When Jesus appeared to him, he made an absolute judgment: "My Lord and my God." He was convinced, once and forever.

The third thought is this: *Jesus pronounces a blessing on all of us, who, generations later, would believe on the basis of the word of others.*

Jesus said to Thomas, "Because you have seen Me, have you believed? Blessed are they who did not see, and yet believed" (John 20:29).

In effect, Jesus recognized how difficult it is to believe. Faith in Christ is no simple thing; it's a miracle, a work of God's grace in the heart.

Think about it. On what basis have you believed in Christ? Because a friend told you? Because you read the Bible? Because you heard a powerful sermon? Because you read a book? Because someone came up to you on the street?

Ultimately, the reason you believe now is on the basis of the experience and words of a few people who saw Jesus in person. That's a slender stick to stake your life and eternity to, and yet, it's what we all do. On the basis of sixty-six texts that have survived centuries of abuse, rebuke, and persecution; on the basis of a book that has been passed along through the ages, you and I have come to the conclusion that Jesus Christ is the Lord of life, the Master of history, and the Purseholder of our destinies. That's remarkable. But it speaks worlds about the power of God's Word and the Holy Spirit.

That's why Jesus pronounces a blessing on all of us. He knew how great the struggle would be.

You know, I look at Thomas and I realize how slight—yet intensely strong—is the thread that holds you and me to the kingdom of God. It's faith. Belief. Conviction. It's something inside us that we can't even explain. It's been put there by the Spirit of God as a gift—His gift to us. With it we purchase heaven, life, eternity, sonship, redemption, salvation, love, joy, peace, hope—everything. It's something so marvelous and so precious that even now I find myself moved to my soul. What God hath wrought in us! What He has given! With faith, we can conquer anything, even disillusionment. Without it, we're weakened corks on a hurricaned sea.

Do You Have It?

So do you have it? Faith? That's the key.

If you have it, use it. Express it. Affirm once again your conviction, your faith in God.

If you don't have it, stop now and ask yourself, "What is it that I need from God to make me have it?" Proof? There's a whole Bible full of proof if you'll only read it. Turning from sin? Then turn.

Whatever it is, seek that faith that falls at Jesus' feet and cries, "My Lord and my God." That, and that alone, will be enough to help you see your way clear through any shattered plan or dream.

4/STILL WAITING AFTER ALL THOSE YEARS

A leader was fired at a church. People quickly took sides. Petitions were signed. Arguments raged in every corner.

The board thought things would calm down. "Just hold steady. Stand firm. Time heals all wounds."

Things didn't calm down. A year later there was still bitterness. Two years later it was still unforgotten. In the midst of it all, some people were saying, "How long will this go on? Why doesn't God do something?"

A fourth kind of disillusionment comes from the problem of time—when a situation goes on and on without change or respite. We see no end in sight. We suffer a problem, go to Scripture, and claim a promise. We wait for fulfillment with high anticipation. We tell ourselves, "God has to come through. He promised." Time trudges on. Nothing happens. Nothing changes. Soon we're disillusioned and ready to find our own way.

A Biblical Example

Such people aren't alone. A great saint of old had the same problem: Abraham.

Remember what God promised him? A son by barren Sarah. He would be a father of nations and she the mother. God gave him that promise at the age of seventy-five (Genesis 12). Sarah was sixty-five. She'd been barren all through their marriage. But Abraham (then Abram) was just starting out on the life of faith. God could do anything. So he left Ur and headed out to this new land God would give him.

What did Abraham think would happen?

It was simple. In a few months or so Sarah would conceive. Nine months later, a son.

What Abraham didn't know was that God had another timetable. In fact, it would be twenty-four years before she conceived. That's a terrific time problem, especially if you're trudging through those twenty-four years one day at a time.

"But God promised a son!"

Correct. But He didn't say when. Abraham assumed that he knew God's timing. And frequently, that's precisely what we do with a a promise from God. *We* attach a timetable to it. That's where disillusionment can strike.

Strangely enough, a promise is often the starting place for disillusionment. For Abraham this was a direct, verbal promise from God: "I will make you a great nation, and I will bless you, and make your name great" (Genesis 12:2). There was no mistaking it. In order to be a great nation, he had to have a son or sons. God promised that he'd have those descendants, presumably through his wife, Sarah.

It's startling how often Christians can be set on the path of disillusionment by a promise they're certain God has made to them. The Christian businessman claims a verse and assures himself God will build his company so that he can give thousands of dollars to missions. The pregnant wife and her husband rely on the fact that God will give them a healthy, whole child. A young couple, just married, cannot imagine that things might not go well for their marriage. When they reach the point of divorce, they're not only bitter at one another, but at God. "How could you let this happen, Lord?"

Often these ideas are rooted in Scripture. "I came that they might have life, and might have it abundantly" (John 10:10). We reason, "Well, abundant life consists in (name your obsession); therefore, Jesus must be planning to give me that."

We claim Romans 8:28 during a perilous situation that strikes our home. So we confidently wait to see the good He'll bring. When He doesn't, we slump into disillusionment, claiming He's not true to His Word, or worse, that He's not real after all.

What we must remember (and that which Abraham didn't) is that God doesn't fulfill all His promises in one week. We can claim them, but we also need to give Him time to work. Sometimes that work may be many years of toil and struggle. Sometimes we have to realize that God's time is not our time; His ideas are not our ideas. We also have to realize that it's for *His* purposes, not ours. And the fulfillment may never come just as we imagined it would.

Into the Land

Returning to Abraham, we notice that he obeyed God. He arrived with his family, his belongings, and his faith intact (Genesis 15). He believed fervently that God would do all He said He would. That becomes a second principle about timetable disillusionment: *disillusioned people often start out being completely obedient.* They're often the more committed kind of Christians. They're zealous. They give all.

But it's this very commitment that often gets them into trouble. Our depraved souls begin to tell us that because we're so committed and obedient, we deserve special attention from God.

Apparently God decided to test Abraham and see precisely how much he did believe. He let a famine strike Canaan.

What happened? Abraham failed the test. Instead of trusting God, he journeyed to Egypt and then lied about Sarah being his wife (Genesis 12). He talked her into saying she was his sister. Because she was beautiful, Abraham thought some powerful overlord might decide to kill him to get her.

Clearly, God had promised to make of Abraham a great nation and to bless him. But what was this? Famine? Disaster? Lying? I'm sure Abraham stopped and mused, "Lord? I thought you were going to bless me."

This is the point at which disillusionment can carve a niche in the soul. God's testing befuddles us. "I thought you were supposed to bless me, Lord. But everything has gone wrong. I thought your promise said . . . . "

Thus, we come to the conclusion God has reneged. He won't follow through on what He said. Or He can't. We begin to feel cheated and hurt, discouraged and disillusioned.

Years Pass

Time went on as Abraham became firmly settled in the land of Hebron. Ten years passed, Abraham experienced more tests and even passed a few. But the one test—believing that God would give him a son through Sarah—was eroding his will. "When will God make it happen?" he began to ask himself. He was eighty-five years old now. And Sarah wasn't getting any younger. How could God make a promise and not fulfill it in ten years? There had to be something wrong.

He and Sarah must have discussed this often. Finally, she suggested an alternative. Maybe God didn't mean the son would come directly through her; perhaps it would happen through another means.

In those days, there was a common parental loophole of the day that she suggested: Have the child through a servant. It was legitimate by traditional terms, even if it wasn't by God's terms.

Abraham thought about it. Perhaps he'd gotten tired of waiting by then. Perhaps his mind flamed with doubts. Whatever he reasoned, he agreed to try it.

This unearths another principle about timetable disillusionment: *In our darkness we often resort to taking things into our own hands.* We have to do something, so why not this? God hasn't fulfilled His promises. We'll just take our own action.

It makes sense, doesn't it? "If you can't beat Him, try a nuclear device."

That's not far from what Abram did. For, by impregnating Hagar and having her give birth to Ishmael, Abraham started the internecine conflict that still rages today between the Arabs and the Jews. After Hagar had Ishmael, a rivalry erupted between Hagar and her mistress. Hagar exalted herself over Sarah because the latter couldn't have children. So Sarah took action and drove Hagar out into the wilderness.

Things Go Downhill

Still, it got worse. Time sped on and no pregnancy arrived. Abraham decided he would accept Ishmael as the heir and waited for death.

Nonetheless, twenty-four years after the initial promise, God appeared to Abraham again and informed him that now the time was right. In one year, Sarah would bear a son (Genesis 17:21).

Yet, what was Abraham's response to God's reassurance? "Oh that Ishmael might live before Thee!" (Genesis 17:18). Abraham was so disillusioned at this point that he tried to talk God out of it! It was as though Abraham was pleading, "Please don't do this to me, Lord. I can't take the waiting. Let's just settle on Ishmael as the heir. It hurts too much to believe that what you're saying could come true."

God waited.

A few weeks later, He visited Abraham again in the form of a man (or possibly an angel). Again, he assured Abraham he'd have a son through Sarah.

Probably Abraham felt a twinge of hope at God's message, but his faith was weak. He was disillusioned, unhappy, and restless. He journeyed through the desert and encountered another king who liked Sarah's looks. Again, he resorted to his old charade of pretending she was his sister. And Abimelech took her as his wife.

An Astonishing Experience

Now it is at this point that an amazing thing happened. God "closed fast all the wombs of the household of Abimelech" (Genesis 20:18), and chose a dream as His way of warning this king not to cohabit with Sarah (Genesis 20:1-7).

Isn't that interesting, considering that infertility was precisely the same problem Sarah had?

So how did God free the king and his household from this punishment? Through Abraham. He told Abraham to pray that God would heal Abimelech, his wife, and his maids. Abraham prayed, their wombs were opened, and they again bore children.

It was a remarkable object lesson for Abraham. Suddenly he saw clearly that it was God who opened and closed wombs. And I believe it was at this point that Abraham began to fulfill the words of Romans 4:18-21, where Paul says, "In hope against hope he believed, in order that he might become a father of many nations." For the first time in twenty-four years he believed completely that God would do what He had promised. And at that point, God opened Sarah's womb.

Finding a Way

This becomes another principle for this brand of disillusionment: *God will find a way even when we can't* Nothing is impossible for Him. Even when all is lost for us, with God it's only a starting place. He planned it that way from the beginning. Why? To gain greater glory for Himself, yes. But also, from our point of view, to lead us into the deepest currents of faith and trust. What builds faith more than getting into a river from which there is no exit, and then seeing God show the way out?

I don't mean that whatever you're waiting for God to do will automatically come true some day. But that what will happen is God's best. *His* plan will come to fruition in your life, and even if it doesn't include your grand plans, it will be right.

In March of 1812, William Carey and two of his missionary associates in India suffered a severe setback. A raging fire swept through their compound. They lost most of the type used to print Bengali Bibles. Most of their Indian versions of the Bible also perished. A Bengali dictionary that had taken years to compile was obliterated. The fire consumed much of the vital equipment used for the work of printing and translation. It was a complete disaster.

Prime ground for disillusionment. But Carey didn't waver. He claimed Romans 8:28 and 29—and waited. A few months later they saw God's answer. When their English supporters received word of the disaster, a spiritual fire swept over England. Thousands of pounds in financial support were raised. New zeal for missions inflamed multitudes. The work in India received a boost upward that they might never have gained otherwise. Where there was no hope, God not only rekindled hope, but He also released His power. Their faith grew.

The Marvelous Journey

What a marvelous adventure for William Carey! And for Abraham. For the latter, it was nearly twenty-five years of festering disillusionment. Yet, God, through His awesome plan and grace, brought him back to reality. He would have a son—and through Sarah. A year later, he did. Isaac was born.

Do you find that time is often a great cause of

disillusionment in your life? God has made a promise; you've claimed it; but He hasn't done it. Yet.

You have a legitimate need. You've prayed and Scripture seems to support your case. But God doesn't answer. And time passes.

Perhaps you're experiencing a severe problem. You've tried all sorts of solutions—the problem persists.

God doesn't want time to become a faith-destroyer. David said, "Wait for the Lord; be strong, and let your heart take courage; yes, wait for the Lord" (Psalm 27:14). James 5:7-8 tell us, "Be patient, therefore, brethren, until the coming of the Lord. Behold, the farmer waits for the precious produce of the soil, being patient about it, until it gets the early and late rains. You too be patient; strengthen your hearts, for the coming of the Lord is at hand."

God doesn't want us to become disillusioned because He's not on our timetable; He wants us to trust that He knows where He's taking us. "For I am confident of this very thing, that He who began a good work in you will perfect it until the day of Christ Jesus" (Philippians 1:6).

The question for us is what do we do with our disillusionment? Resort to our own means? Or go to God and seek His help, His love, His assurance?

We can let time crush our hearts. Or we can come to the place of complete trust and confidence. God is faithful—even when we're not.

5/On The Shelf Gathering Dust

Things were going well. Several young people in the group for which I was youth pastor were growing and becoming more committed to Christ. They'd even started their own Bible study for their local high school friends. It was flourishing. I only wished we could transpose the good things happening there to the youth at church.

But I was confident. I went to that adult youth leaders' meeting full of energy and hope. When I arrived, everyone was there already. That was unusual.

Then, moments after I sat down, I noticed a strange discomfort. But I said nothing. Larry, one of the elders, spoke first. "We've called this meeting to discuss some critical problems we're facing, Mark. We're very concerned about the youth ministry here at church."

I nodded. I already knew that.

Then he floored me. "Mark, we feel—all of us,"—he motioned to the three others sitting before me—"that it's come down to an important decision. In short, we think you ought to begin looking for another job."

Instantly, my heart began racing. Anger, confusion, frustration all tangled up in my mind. What had I done? Why was there no warning? I could barely stammer, "You don't want me to continue here as youth pastor?"

Carl broke in. He and I had had disagreements before. He said, "It's not that, Mark. We just feel the church's vision and yours don't match. We don't feel you fit in here the way we'd like."

"Then you want me to resign?" I felt as though I might begin hyperventilating.

"Not at all," said Carl. "We just want you to look for a new job. Take as long as you need. We don't want to pressure you."

Pressure me? Then what was this? I felt destroyed inside. Why hadn't they at least given me a warning?

The next morning I turned in a letter of resignation. It was a foolish act of anger and bitterness, but I felt it was the only dignity I had left.

The announcement shocked the youth group, and many tried to start a movement not to accept my resignation. For a moment that encouraged me, but I realized causing trouble wasn't the answer. The elders quietly accepted my resignation a few days later. I decided to leave without a fuss. That was, perhaps, my only intelligent move in the whole debacle.

For the next nine months, I despondently looked for another ministry. But I was single, without solid recommendations, and minus a strong track record. Fortunately, a small church came along in need of a pastor. Ten months after my resignation I had a new job.

But that ten months in between was agony. It was not according to my plans at all. I was supposed—in my mind— to launch a successful youth ministry, have a church discover me and ask me to be their pastor, then ride off into the sunset in the wake of a tremendous pulpit ministry that converted thousands.

But God wasn't following my plan. He had His own in mind, and His would prevail.

Nonetheless, I frequently felt disillusioned with myself, with the ministry, with the Lord. Almost daily I cried out in my prayers, "Lord, why did you let this happen to me? Did I receive a call to the ministry, get a master's degree, and seek only to serve you for this?"

Set On The Shelf

The expression we use is "being set on the shelf." There are many reasons it happens: personal sin, a mistake of judgment, persecution, incompetence, unnecessary roughness by elders in churches, revenge, an illness. But it happens. The average stay of the average pastor is less than three years in churches today. Firings are frequent. A friend who had this happen to him wrote me, "The waiting is sheer agony."

Set on the shelf. Gathering dust. A bookend. Forgotten.

But it's not just something that happens to pastors and people in the ministry. It also happens to laymen in every facet of life. Perhaps you were the dynamic leader of a large Sunday School class, but you had to move to another town. Now you just can't seem to find a place of service.

Or maybe you once had a top echelon job in a fine corporation. You spoke frequently to Christian groups. And then the impossible happened: your company was bought out, and you were dismissed in the aftermath.

Or maybe you've been a real force in your community. You led many to Christ as you spread the good news. But something happened, something changed. You witness. But there are no conversions. You detect a hardness of heart. The days of success are gone.

Have you been any of these folks? The feelings of disillusionment in the midst of such a circumstance can be overpowering. Doubts assail you. You feel discouraged, depressed, lonely, wishing for some action, something different. You wonder if God has forgotten you completely.

And that's another issue: God. There may be anger inside of you toward Him, and you don't know what to do with it. "Why did you let this happen to me, Lord? Don't you care?"

There were plenty of people in Scripture that God set on the shelf—for a season.

Jacob – during those long lonely years after the loss of Joseph (Genesis 37).

Joseph – first a slave, then a convict (Genesis 37).

Samson – in prison with his eyes destroyed (Judges 16).

King Saul – after the Spirit departed from him (I Samuel 28).

Jeremiah – when he was cast into a muddy cistern (Jeremiah 38).

John the Baptist – after Herod imprisoned him (Matthew 11,14).

Even Jesus lived in obscurity the first thirty years of His life (Luke 3).

But there's one person I always turn to when I feel like I'm on the shelf—Moses. He committed a horrid error that led to even more horrible inner turmoil and agony. He murdered an Egyptian, then ran into the wilderness and spent the next forty years convinced he was incompetent, unable to do anything good for God or His people. Forty years in obscurity. Forty years of 24 hour days studded with sighs, wishes, regrets, and painful reminders. Forty years, perhaps, of telling himself he was good for nothing, a fool, an incompetent, a weakling . . . a murderer.

Let's look at his situation in more detail .

A Short History of a Long Disillusionment

Moses began life on the down side of Israelite history (Exodus 1–2). The whole nation lived in slavery in Egypt. Because they were so numerous, Pharaoh decided to stop the explosion by killing all the male children. Moses' parents kept him for three months, but then decided to take a risk. His mother put him in a basket covered with tar and placed him in the Nile at a point somewhere above the place she knew Pharaoh's daughter bathed. Sure enough, the baby's boat cruised straight for the spot. Pharaoh's daughter had him fished out and promptly made him a son. Then she hired Moses' own mother as a wet nurse, and Moses grew up in Pharaoh's palace.

He must have known about his heritage, and sometime around forty he began watching his enslaved brethren. One day he caught an Egyptian taskmaster beating one of the Jews. Moses took action. He killed the Egyptian and hid him in the sand. Clearly, Moses had determination. He was physically strong. And he possessed a genuine concern for the Hebrews.

With his murderous act behind him, Moses felt a greater sense of confidence about delivering Israel from slavery. The next day when he went out, he saw two Hebrews fighting. He tried to intercede and stop them.

Immediately, they denounced him (probably not realizing he was also a Hebrew). "Who made you a prince or a judge over us? Are you intending to kill me, as you did the Egyptian?" (Exodus 2:14).

Instantly, Moses knew he was in trouble. His murderous deed had become common knowledge. Undoubtedly many of the Hebrews were talking about it. In a short time, the Egyptians would know.

When Pharaoh did hear of it, he knew Moses could never function as a king of Egypt. He was loyal to Israel, not Egypt, so Pharaoh tried to kill him.

But Moses fled across the Nile into the land of Midian. This was a journey of over 200 miles, all the way across the Sinai Peninsula to what is now Saudi Arabia.

Moses settled down to the life of a shepherd. He married Zipporah, the daughter of Jethro, the priest of Midian. How he dealt with his act of murder is not clear. But from his conversation with God in Exodus 3 and 4, we can deduce several truths about the nature of his discouragement in being set on the shelf.

1. Total loss of confidence.

God told him He'd seen the condition of His people. He wanted to rescue them. He wanted to send Moses to Pharaoh to bring them out of Egypt.

What was Moses' reply? It's the classic answer of utter inferiority: "Who am I, that I should go to Pharaoh, and that I should bring the sons of Israel out of Egypt?" (Exodus 3:11). The rhetorical expression here is one of utter personal contempt. "Who am I? Nobody. No one. Zilch. Zip. Zero." He had no confidence in his abilities. Once he was somebody. But now he was this shepherd in Nowheresville. What was that? He'd muffed his opportunity to deliver the Israelites.

2. Inability to cope with the simplest of problems.

After God assured Moses He'd be with him, Moses looked for another excuse. He was wriggling now, but he said, "Behold, I am going to the sons of Israel, and I shall say to them, 'The God of your fathers has sent me to you.' Now they may say to me, 'What is His name?' What shall I say to them?" (Exodus 3:13).

The disillusioned person sees life's simplest problems as hopeless boggles.

But I don't think Moses asked the question to gain information. It was a way to get out of the situation. He didn't care whether or not God had a name, and whether or not the Hebrews would recognize it. All he saw was the problem of credibility. He didn't want to have to face that.

3. An intolerable fear of rejection.

The third component of Moses' discouragement is found in his reaction to God's third reply. "What if they will not believe me, or listen to what I say? For they may say, 'The Lord has not appeared to you'" (Exodus 4:1).

A tough problem indeed. How could he prove it? In his own mind they had disqualified him as the savior of Israel forty years ago. Why, now that he wasn't even a member of

Pharaoh's household, only a powerless shepherd, would they listen to him? Moses couldn't see a reason.

But his problems were deeper than need of a reason to believe; he feared rejection.

When God pulls you out of the mainstream and puts you on a shelf somewhere in Timbucktu, you become afraid of losing even what you do have.

4. He felt incompetent

God gave Moses two miracles he could command at will: his staff turning into a serpent and his hand becoming leprous. But they weren't enough. Moses dredged up a fourth excuse. "Please, Lord, I have never been eloquent, neither recently, nor in time past, nor since Thou hast spoken to Thy servant; for I am slow of speech and slow of tongue" (Exodus 4:10).

Moses saw himself as a feeble public speaker. No one would pay attention to him. He felt incompetent. If there was one thing he knew, it was this: anyone who was going to negotiate with Pharaoh, stir up Israel, and win their freedom, had to be quickwitted, sharp, and slick with his lips.

Still, God encouraged Moses again, assuring him it was He who made the tongue and He knew precisely how to work with Moses to teach him to speak (4:11-12). But it still wasn't enough.

5. The "anyone but me" syndrome.

Moses was unchanged. He couldn't do the job. His disillusionment with himself was so overwhelming that he simply refused to go. He said to God, "Please, Lord, now send the message by whomever Thou wilt" (Exodus 4:13). He meant, "Send it by someone else, not me."

When you're on the shelf, you'd think that your hope would be just to get off. But it's a strange thing. As you get submerged into that environment, lose confidence, develop various fears, and shrink from smaller tasks, you reach a point where you're sure anyone could do it but you.

A man I know was deserted by his wife. For years it was questionable whether she was even a Christian. She remarried. But he struggled with the issue for decades, wondering if God would ever want him to marry again. Scripturally, as I understood it, he had the right to marry. But his conscience wouldn't permit it. Even when he met a widow with whom he fell in love, there was hesitation. He wanted to be sure.

Some of that hesitation, I believe, stemmed from the disillusionment we feel when we're on the shelf. Once we've been there for some time, it's not easy to bound into something which may yield even greater problems.

All these things—feelings of inferiority, fear of rejection, a sense of incompetence—can assault you at that time. When God finally decides to get you back into the mainstream, like Moses, you may balk. God has to take further action. He doesn't want to leave us on the shelf. So what did He do in Moses' case?

God Acts

For the person mired in disillusionment, I see five elements of God's rehabilitation program.

First, He let Moses sit until He was ready.

Waiting is agony for most of us. One of my professors used to call us "GoGo Boys." We want to move, to get out there and do it.

But God does things methodically. Not at the right time. At the perfect time.

How was letting Moses stay in Midian for forty years the right time? It's hard to tell from the record. But several things are clear. First, God waited until the Pharaoh in whose house Moses was raised was dead. Second, he let Moses gain the maturity only time and trouble can bring—eighty years worth. Third, in that forty years, Moses' brother had also matured. He would be indispensable in the process of leading. Fourth, several of Moses' most important men—Joshua particularly—were babies when Moses left Egypt as a fugitive. They needed to grow up, too. But fifth, and most importantly, when God first called Moses, He told him, "I have surely seen the affliction of My people who are in Egypt, and have given heed to their cry . . . " (Exodus 3:7). Perhaps it was only after Moses reached eighty that the people had begun to cry out to God, their God, the living God, for deliverance.

Whatever God's reasons for Moses' forty year stint in Midian, His timing was perfect. When God acts, there is success. But when Moses took his own actions, there was nothing but failure.

Second, He dealt with Moses' objections.

Each of the Mosaic excuses was answered by divine exhortation.

Think about it. What if your boss at work asks you to do a certain job? Do you make excuses and try to get out of it? Maybe once. Maybe twice. But three strikes and you're probably fired.

Now in Moses' situation, this isn't just a boss. This is God.

And Moses stands there and tries to excuse himself out of it!

It's astonishing.

But what's even more incredible is that God takes the time to answer. Like a kindly father trying to teach his baby boy to toddle, God keeps coming back, encouraging, boosting, promoting.

I love that. Most of us would have whammed Moses out of the running after his second bleat. But not God. He keeps working, helping, uplifting. He never gives up, no matter how lame or useless the person may seem.

Third, He gave him a push.

When Moses balked, God didn't. He supplied the soothing words that would help jar this soggy prophet out of his mire. When the prophet still refused, He gave an order no one could refuse. (See Exodus 4:14-17.) Moses requested, "God, please find someone else." And God rejoined, "Someone else, huh? All right, there's your brother Aaron. He speaks fluently. As a matter of fact, he's headed this way now to meet you. You tell him what I tell you. And I'll be with both of your mouths. Got it? Now get your staff, and get going!"

The person mired in disillusionment needs a shove now and then.

Martin Luther was once so depressed and disillusioned, his wife, Katherine von Bora, dressed in funeral black. "Why are you dressed in black?" exclaimed Luther. "Has someone died?"

"Oh, yes," said his wife. "God."

"God died? Have you gone mad, woman?"

"No, the way you were moping about and so depressed, I felt sure God Himself must have died."

Luther popped out of it.

A push. A jab. A shove. We all need it now and then. The disillusioned person needs it most.

Fourth, He developed Moses spiritually step by step.

Moses' story in Scripture is all the more remarkable when you study how God took this cowering shepherd and turned him into a lion. Read Exodus 3 through 14. You'll reach the climactic moment in Exodus 14:13. There, Moses stands on the edge of the Red Sea. Water before him. The Egyptians in their weapon-bristled chariots behind him. Panicking Hebrews all around him. But what does the weak-kneed, lily-liver of Exodus 3 and 4 do? He bounds onto a rock, raises his staff, and booms, "Do not fear! Stand by and see the salvation of the Lord which He will accomplish for you today!"

And this was before Moses knew what God planned to do! He had no inkling that God would part the Red Sea. The one thing he did know: God wasn't about to desert them. He who had decimated Egypt with the ten plagues wouldn't waver now. Moses had confidence. His disillusionment was gone. He knew God could do anything.

And God did. He parted the sea. Israel walked through on dry land. The Eygptians drowned.

How did all this happen? Where did this Moses come from? He's certainly not the same character we saw in Exodus 3-4.

That's right. God had transformed him. He had led him step by step. Several times in the chapters following Exodus 3 and 4, Moses ran, gave up, complained, and handed God his resignation. But God stood with him and developed him.

I'm convinced that anyone who suffers from this kind of disillusionment has every reason to rejoice. God plans to transform him and his life—if he'll just let Him do it!

That's God's way. To whom did Paul go? Not to his own kind, the Pharisees—but to the Gentiles, the very people he had been taught to hate most on earth. To whom did Peter go? Not the Galileans, the fishermen types he might identify with—but the sophisticated Jews of Jerusalem. All God needs is a willing heart. With that, He can take it anywhere.

Moses discovered that. God used his disillusionment and transformed him.

Fifth, God kept His word.

One of the main problems the disillusioned person has is that he feels God has let him down. The Word isn't true. Those lofty promises—forget it, they're false. God just doesn't keep His word.

Indeed, it can look that way—especially if we make His Word say things it doesn't, and primarily if we have egos that think God should do for us what He will not do for others.

But with Moses, as with everyone, God kept His word to the letter. Everything He said would happen happened. Everything He promised came to pass. In fact, in the book of Joshua, when the people finally came into the land of milk and honey, Joshua wrote, "Not one of the good promises which the Lord had made to the house of Israel failed; all came to pass" (Joshua 21:45).

God's promises are firm although not always fast. Not in our timing. Not according to our expectations. But according to His thoughts, His plans, His decrees.

At the beginning of this chapter I spoke of my own disillusionment at having to leave my position as a youth pastor under pressure. For the next nine months I looked for a ministry, but no one wanted me. I felt deserted, forgotten, a dreg. Moreover, I was angry at God for allowing me to fail so completely.

But one thing sustained me. Several young people who had been in the youth group at the church wrote me consistently. Their letters were full of the happenings at the church. But more importantly, they spoke of my ministry to them. It was as though the Lord Himself was doing this to keep me afloat when all I wanted to do was sink. The disillusionment passed when I did enter another ministry and began to see God's success in preaching and teaching. It wasn't to prove those others wrong. It was a reaffirmation. God was reassuring me, telling me that my call to the ministry hadn't been a mistake, that He was leading me every step of the journey.

God is not in the business of leaving people on the shelf. He may set them there for study and inspection, maybe even a little fermentation. But not forever. Not without making it clear why. Not without fulfilling the rest of His plan.

6/Oh, For The Good Old Days

"It wasn't like this when I was a kid."

"Ah, those were the days, weren't they, Mabel?"

"You should've heard Pastor O'Reilly. Now he could preach. Not like these whippersnappers today."

Ever heard those words plop out of a parent, grandparent, elder, or older friend? They speak of what happened "way back when," and the now suddenly shrivels up. The sparkle of today runs into gray. The bright jewel of tomorrow splinters into a cracked glass.

We call the then, "The good old days." We call the now, "Hard times." It can be a source of powerful pain and remorse.

This is a sixth brand of discouragement common among Christians. It's the kind that happens when the past begins to look so much better than the present.

A variation on it is comparing someone else's work down the street to yours up on Hard Times Avenue. Why are they prospering and you're not? What makes them deserve God's blessing and not you?

Comparing the past to the present, or others to yourself, can make you feel like a wretch. You simply don't measure up.

A Biblical Example

Israel discovered this after their exile in Babylon. They returned to Judah during the days of Ezra. Later, Nehemiah arrived and helped the exiles rebuild the walls of Jerusalem. The people built homes of cedar, slouched back into their easy chairs, and plucked figs for snacks. Everything was great.

But then a prophet named Haggai arrived on the scene. He spoke with Zerubbabel, the governor of Judah, and warned him about a conspicuous problem: God's temple still lay in ruins. "Thus says the Lord of hosts, 'This people says, "The time has not come, even the time for the house of the Lord to be rebuilt"'"(Haggai 1:2). Haggai rebuked the people severely. They lolled about in their panelled homes and passed their days in leisure while the temple didn't have two stones piled square.

God told them to consider their ways. "Why do you think you sow much and harvest little?" He asked. "Why do you drink but can't get drunk? Why do you put on clothing, but can't seem to get warm" (1:6)?

The answer was obvious: because God was disciplining them about the temple. They had spent all their money and time on themselves. But it was God who had brought them out of exile and returned them to the land. Had they already forgotten?

The people had become complacent, uncaring. God was far off, a dot on the horizon of their consciousness.

But now that Haggai had stomped in with his verbal blowtorch, some new fires were ignited in hearts. The exiles set about rebuilding the temple. Soon they had a place in which to worship God.

A place, yes. After all, for over seventy years they'd had nothing. But it wasn't much of a place. There were still a few among them who remembered the old temple, the Temple of Solomon, one of the seven wonders of the world in its day.

The Talk

You can almost hear the conversation from some of the

older gents and ladies who remembered that Temple.

"Don't look much like Solomon's Temple," says Jehu.

"Well, we did the best we could," retorts young Abraham.

Jehu pokes his cane into the dirt. "If that's our best, I'd hate to see our worst."

Abraham clenches his fists. "If you think you can do better, do it."

Jehu shakes his head. "You young fellows are the ones to take care of it. I'm just an old fellow. I've already put in my years. And I'm telling you, this temple is nothing. Hear me? Nothing. It's a heap. I should have died in Babylon for seeing this. It makes my heart sick."

The younger men are all angry now. "Well what was so great about Solomon's Temple anyway?"

"First of all, it was big," says Jehu. "This thing's a box. I'm ashamed to go in."

"We don't have that much stone."

"Stone! Pooh! Solomon used quarry stone, my boy. Good stone. Beautiful, white, costly. Lots of shekels poured into it. No expense was too great. But this? Just look at it. We groped around in the fields to find stones for this. Pitiful."

The young men hang their heads.

"And another thing, fellows, when Solomon built the Lord's Temple—I call that one the Lord's temple because this one, well, what can I say? Anyway—he didn't allow a single hammer in the place. It was all prepared at the quarry. I tell you, it was a master job."

He pauses and looks at the new temple, then shakes his head. "It's a pitied shame, men. A shame. I don't even want to worship there. I tell you, I think Jehovah Himself wouldn't even want to come down in His glory and reside here."

Everyone's totally discouraged now. The old days so outshone the new days, there was no reason even to hope.

The Good Days

The "good old days" can be a source of tremendous pain for one stuck in the midst of today's calamity.

The first year after I became a Christian was the greatest, most thrilling year of my life up to that point. I led several people to the Lord. I worked in Vermont as a short order chef and snow-skied all week. I received a call to ministry. I worked the following summer in an evangelistic center on the boardwalk in Wildwood, New Jersey, preached my first message, and got accepted—despite terrific odds and a late application—to Dallas Theological Seminary. I was sure such a year was unbeatable.

Yet, my second year as a Christian was even better. I went to Dallas, studied under some of the world's greatest theological professors and public speakers, and led more people to the Lord. I joined a singing group, taught Sunday School, received money in the mail when I needed it, and seemed to be seeing a miracle a day.

That summer I returned to the evangelistic center in Wildwood as one of the staff and had even greater experiences. At the end I told the Lord, "Things couldn't get better."

Nonetheless, my third year as a Christian was even more incredible. My coursework continued to go well. I was learning to preach. My grades were the highest they'd ever been. I was rated as a top Sunday School teacher. And that summer I was a pastoral intern at a church in Hershey, Pennsylvania which had grown from a group of twenty-five to over a thousand in four years. The people there loved me and I loved them. I was sure the Lord could never outdo this. And yet, by now, I was prepared for nothing but wonders.

That fourth year was the year I crashed. A two-and-half year biochemical depression banged into my life. The chute opened and I dropped through. I felt for the first time as though God didn't even exist. That was when I began thinking about the "good old days." I forgot about the struggles I'd had in those first years. I forgot about the sin problems, the family problems, the girl problems. Suddenly, I was totally disillusioned and spent most of my time wishing the past would somehow reassert itself.

I wonder if that wasn't where Israel was in Haggai's day.

After the people rebuilt the temple, some of the exiles remembered Solomon's Temple, one of the greatest temples of the east. When they compared the rebuilt version to that one, the present temple looked dismal.

God Confronted the Problem

But God in His wisdom confronted the problem frontally. He saw their fear and their disillusionment. But He didn't want them mired in that condition. Through Haggai we learn several strong principles about the "good old days."

First, the issue is whether God is with us now, not what He did in others then.

Notice what God says to the people through Haggai: " 'Who is left among you who saw this temple in its former glory? And how do you see it now? Does it not seem to you like nothing in comparison? But now take courage, Zerubbabel;' declares the Lord; 'take courage,' declares the Lord, 'and work; for I am with you,' says the Lord of hosts" (Haggai 2:3-4). God confronts the situation directly. "All right, granted the temple doesn't look as good as the former one. Work anyway. For I am with you. Just as much as I was with the others when they built that temple, so I am with you."

Ever look at the achievements of people in the past and think you can never equal them? Peter's sermon on the day of Pentecost when 3,000 were saved. Paul roaming over the entire Roman world, planting churches, and turning whole cities upside down. The miracles that occurred. People like Martin Luther, John Calvin, John Wesley, George Whitefield, Charles Spurgeon, Dwight Moody. Who can equal them?

You know what? It doesn't matter. If God is with you now, and He chooses to accomplish deeds through you which are less than stupendous, what is that to you? He'll reward you on the basis of obedience, not results.

Remember the woman who gave the two mites (Mark 12:41-44)? That was equivalent to 1/8 of a cent today. Then, it was 1/128th of a denarius. A denarius was one day's wage for a typical laborer. If you consider one day's wage at eight dollars an hour to be sixty-four dollars, that means the woman's gift was the equivalent of one-half dollar. How much could that buy today in terms of evangelistic ministry?

Yet, Jesus commended the widow for having put in more than all the others combined. Why? Because her heart was right. God was with her. He could take that half dollar and turn it into something far greater. What if that widow's mites were used to pay a scribe who was copying a scroll of Isaiah? That scroll might have gone on to be read by thousands of others. Paul himself might have used that scroll in his teaching. Hundreds, perhaps thousands of people might have come to Christ through the repetition of those words from Isaiah. All that's to say nothing of the effect of the widow's example on those who read the Bible now.

The fact that God is always with His children makes everything else superfluous. What did Paul say? Read Philippians 3. All his achievements, which to Jews were paramount, were nothing next to "knowing Christ Jesus my Lord" (Philippians 3:8). What matters is not how much we do for God, but that God is involved in everything we do!

Second, when God is with us, we have no reason to fear or to be disillusioned.

Look at Haggai 2:5: "As for the promise which I made you

when you came out of Egypt, My Spirit is abiding in your midst; do not fear." Charles Ryrie, in the *Ryrie Study Bible*, includes a note which refers to the promises God made to Israel when they came out of Egypt. They are found in Exodus 19:5, 29:45-46, and 33:14. Each of those texts refers to the fact that Israel was God's possession and that He dwelt among them.

What that says to me is that it isn't the size of your church, who you're sitting next to in the pew, or how many kids are in your Sunday School class, but whether God is there, being honored and in charge of what's happening.

When the disciples came back from their first evangelistic crusade under Jesus' direction, they rejoiced and said, "Lord, even the demons are subject to us in Your name." Jesus replied, "Do not rejoice in this, that the spirits are subject to you, but rejoice that your names are recorded in heaven" (Luke 10:17,20). What matters is not the power we wield, but that we know the Person who gives the power.

Third, what matters is our fitting into God's plans.

When I was in Little League, I wanted to pitch. Unfortunately, I wasn't much of a pitcher. My coach put me on third base, though he did try me several times on the mound. At one point he said to me, "Look, do you want the team to win? Then your job is to play where I put you, and play your best. What matters is winning, not you doing what you want."

It was a strange idea at the time, especially to a member of the 60s "me" generation. We've been taught all our lives to do our own thing, and if it feels right to do it. After becoming a Christian, I found that I had to adopt a new mentality, to become not just a team player, but God's player.

Notice what God said to the Israelites: "For thus says the Lord of hosts, 'Once more in a little while, I am going to shake the heavens and earth, the sea also and the dry land. And I will shake all the nations, and they will come with the wealth of all nations; and I will fill this house with glory,' says the Lord of hosts" (Haggai 2:6-7).

God has a plan, and what matters is that we fit in where He put us. If we refuse and go our own way, we may end up with nothing, for God's plan will work out. We may be left behind, doing our own plan and not fitting in at all.

Sometimes it's all perspective. Think of a blacksmith in 1776 at work in his shop shoeing horses for some American soldiers fighting in the Revolution. As he works, he wonders why he has to remain in his shop while others go off to change history. He tells himself how little his work means, and he feels depressed and useless. Suddenly, he notices he misplaced a nail in the shoe. "Oh well," he says to himself, "it's only a nail."

That horse goes out to battle. And because of that nail, the shoe was lost. But when the horse lost his shoe, he went lame, so that horse was lost. But when his mount fell, the rider fell also. And for want of a horse, a rider was lost. Perhaps General Washington needed a fast rider to take a message to a colonel on his left flank. He was looking for a certain rider. But that certain rider had fallen. Washington never got his message to that colonel. And for want of a rider, a battle was lost. And for want of a battle. . .

Well, you know the story. But isn't that the story of all of us? We become disillusioned with where God has put us, so we slack off, thinking our little job—driving nails in horseshoes or teaching the junior boys or preaching to this little group of ladies at this tiny church or taking out the trash after the service on Sundays—doesn't really amount to much. So why do an excellent job or even do it at all?

That's the disillusionment mentality. Shake it, or it will shake you.

Fourth. God's intent is glory.

Look at the last thing God says to the people of Haggai's day: "The silver is Mine, and the gold is Mine. . .'The latter glory of this house will be greater than the former,'. . .'and in this place I shall give peace' " (Haggai 2:8-9). What is God's plan for all peoples of all ages who walk with Him? Glory. *God's* glory.

Paul spoke of God's plan in Romans. "Whom He predestined, these He also called; and whom He called, these He also justified; and whom He justified, these He also glorified" (Romans 8:30). Jesus referred to God's plan in His high priestly prayer of John 17. "And the glory which Thou has given Me I have given to them; that they may be one, just as We are one; I in them, and Thou in Me, that they may be perfected in unity, that the world may know that Thou didst send Me, and didst love them, even as Thou didst love Me" (17:22-23). James said, "Humble yourselves in the presence of the Lord, and He will exalt you" (James 4:10).

Whatever situations, hardships, circumstances, evils, goods, riches, or poverty we endure in this world, ultimately they are nothing compared to what God plans for the next. They are all part of God's plan to conform us to the image of His Son (Romans 8:29). Paul thought of it this way: "For I consider that the sufferings of this present time are not worthy to be compared with the glory that is to be revealed to us" (Romans 8:18). The "latter glory of this house will be greater than the former," Haggai said as he quoted the Lord (2:9). Whatever happened in the "good old days," the grandeur of eternity should overwhelm our vision.

The Worldly Outlook

Those are nice words, but when you're stuck in the nitty-gritty of the here and the now, they're sometimes hard to accept. "I don't care about the future; I care about what's happening today."

But ultimately, that's the cry of worldliness, of being in love with this world. If there's a key to the disillusionment we feel when we think the accomplishments of the past are so much greater than those now, it's the fact that the Lord wants us to set our minds on "things above, not on the things that are on earth" (Colossians 3:2). The Christian is to set his sights on heaven, on Jesus, on eternity, not on his lot in this life. The beauty of the Christian life in the here and now is that we're only passing through. "Strangers and exiles," God calls us (Hebrews 11:13). There's no reason to get down and get comfortable, because we'll soon be moving on. This isn't "home."

Malcolm Muggeridge wrote in *Jesus Rediscovered,* "The only disaster that can befall us, I have come to realize, is to feel ourselves to be home here on earth. As long as we are aliens, we cannot forget our true homeland, which is that other kingdom You proclaimed."

That outlook breaks the gloom of disillusionment and opens the door toward a tomorrow filled with adventure, joy, and triumph.

7/BIG LETDOWN BY YOUR BIG LEADER

Abraham lied about Sarah, saying she was his sister to Pharaoh in Egypt and later to Abimelech, king of Gerar.

Moses murdered an Egyptian and had a serious problem with anger.

Samson lusted after women and finally fell because of Delilah.

Eli failed to discipline his rebellious sons who used God's temple as a means to make money.

King David committed adultery with Bathsheba, murdered her husband, and ultimately suffered the most stinging rebuke a father can suffer: the outrage, rebellion, and destruction of his son, Absalom.

Peter denied he even knew Jesus—three times.

John Mark deserted Paul and Barnabas on the first missionary journey.

Timothy stumbled in the faith. Paul wrote a whole letter to him about it and to encourage him.

Martin Luther persecuted Jews.

John Calvin tried to legislate Christian morality in his home city of Geneva, Switzerland, and was banished.

George Whitefield was obese.

Today, we have headlines that make us cringe. Thousands of others on lesser planes also fail, and their followers are just as pained and ~~~' ~~ ~~ ~~~ir falls.

What words ʊʊ ᴡᴇ ʜᴇaʀ in regard to such people?

Fraud. Hypocrite. Heretic.

A reproach to the name of God.

Blasphemer. Pharisee. Fake.

We have a whole dictionary full of them.

But what is worse is what it does to God's people. Honest, godly, committed Christians have sacrificed their time and money for the likes of the people above. They've given earnestly and sincerely. They've been faithful year in and year out. Some refuse to believe the rumors, then the public spectacles, finally the confessions. In some instances, those folks become profoundly disillusioned. They go away saying things like, "You can't trust anyone anymore." "Even Christians are frauds." "They're no different from anyone else."

And sometimes they say, "I'm finished. No more of this." They leave the church, the ministry, their homes, their lives. They give up. They call it quits. They may not even want to be Christians anymore. For them, faith is meaningless. Admittedly, their eyes were on people not God, but the result is still devastating.

God Said So

The Lord warned us it would be like this.

"Beware of the false prophets, who come to you in sheep's clothing, but inwardly are ravenous wolves. You will know them by their fruits" (Matthew 7:15-16).

"Many false prophets will arise, and will mislead many. . . . For false Christs and false prophets will arise and will show great signs and wonders, so as to mislead, if possible, even the elect" (Matthew 24:11,24).

"I know that after my departure savage wolves will come in among you, not sparing the flock; and from among your own selves men will arise, speaking perverse things, to draw away the disciples after them" (Acts 20:29-30).

"But realize this, that in the last days difficult times will come. For men will be lovers of self, lovers of money, boastful. . . holding to a form of godliness, although they have denied its power" (II Timothy 3:1–25).

"But false prophets also arose among the people, just as there will also be false teachers among you, who will secretly introduce destructive heresies... And many will follow their sensuality, and because of them the way of the truth will be maligned; and in their greed they will exploit you with false words" (II Peter 2:1-3).

"I wrote something to the church, but Diotrephes, who loves to be first among them, does not accept what we say" (III John 9).

"For certain persons have crept in unnoticed, those who were long beforehand marked out for this condemnation, ungodly persons who turn the grace of our God into licentiousness and deny our only Master and Lord, Jesus Christ" (Jude 4).

This is Christ's church. And it's chock full of fakes. I don't mean to suggest that people like Abraham, David or Martin Luther and others weren't born again. But we've been warned. Among our godly, Christ-committed leaders, there are wolves, charlatans, frauds, and, in all cases, ordinary sinners like you and me.

A Process

But how can this be? If this is so, whom can you trust?

Frankly speaking, any Christian who becomes a blind devotee of someone other than Jesus is walking into quicksand. Paul said, "Be imitators of me" on several occasions. But one time he qualified it. "Be imitators of me, just as I also am of Christ" (I Corinthians 11:1). Whomever you follow, whoever teaches you, measure him or her against the person of Christ. Follow only insofar as they reflect the passion, character, and life of Christ.

In my lifetime, there have been several men and women whose writings, messages, and personal character greatly influenced me. I read their books over and over. I listened to their tapes. When I had opportunity, I went to hear them in person.

Reactions to Hypocritical Leaders

Among them, there are a few who fell into sin. Analyzing my own thoughts, I see several reactions I made to such sinful acts. In fact, in such a situation, there are parallels to the grief process that analysts have discovered among those who lose a loved one through death. There are some differences, but I personally see and have experienced five elements.

1. Denial. The obvious first response is a refusal to accept the truth. Whether the information about your leader comes to you through rumor, the media, a letter, or other means, at first we tend to deny it completely. "I can't believe he would do such a thing." "No way—he's a man of God." "It's a lie, a rumor. People are trying to destroy him." The psychic pain of acceptance is too great. We fight it and tell ourselves all sorts of lies to fend it off.

2. "Let's all forgive." When the relentless truth presses itself upon us, we reach a place where we can no longer successfully deny it. It's true. He sinned. Frequently, there's a call for an across the board forgiveness. "Let's all join hands and help him through this. Let's forgive." But there's an important difference between this, and "I forgive." This is not personal. This is done as a group. We're still not dealing with reality. We're simply exhorting everyone else to be magnanimous. It's touched our hearts, but we haven't involved our heads yet. We begin telling everyone that people make mistakes, give the guy a break, let's recognize the sin and go on.

The problem is that, frequently, the leader who has been caught in a blatant fault does not follow the biblical mandate for humility, confession, and repentance. Rather he hedges, faces up only to proven evidence, skirts the issue, dodges, makes up excuses. Seeing the leader do this results in a third element.

3. A sense of betrayal. When we see that our leader (idol?!) has not only sinned but is dealing with his sin deceitfully and unscripturally, we often become angry. When we realize our beloved is resorting to manipulation, lying, excuses, and all the other rubbish involved in attempting to escape a genuine admission of guilt, we feel betrayed. Perhaps we've poured hundreds, thousands of dollars into this person's work and ministry. We've given our time. We've spent hours in prayer. We believed in this leader.

The truth hurts. Something deep within us twists and begins to scream, "I've been had." We realize this leader may not only be a plain brown paper sinner just like us, but worse, he's violating the very scriptural principles he demanded that we obey. We begin to seethe, "Come on, let's see you do what you told us to do." It occurs to us that this beloved leader may be a major hypocrite.

4. Anger. All of this leads to deep, boiling anger. Often, we want to see him "get his."

The classic example of such fierce anger is Absalom, King David's son (II Samuel 11–15). The king had failed in several ways. First, by committing adultery and murder. Next, by not punishing his son Amnon when he raped his half-sister, Tamar. Tamar was Absalom's full sister. When the king did nothing about it, Absalom became outraged and fashioned a plan to kill Amnon. When Amnon was murdered, Absalom fled, and David banished him from his presence.

That was where the disillusionment set in. It involved injustice, personal sin, and a weak will. Absalom became totally disgruntled with his father's leadership, even though David was Israel's greatest king.

5. Rebellion. The final stage of such disillusionment is rank rebellion—an all out rejection of the leader you once revered and with it a rejection of everything he once stood for even if it is Jesus, God, the Bible, Christianity, faith.

It Doesn't Have To Be This Way

Disillusionment with our leaders forms a spiral staircase down to destruction. We tend to think that spiritual leaders have a special hold on holiness. We have a plan for them in our minds, that they'll only succeed and go on to higher and greater successes, vicariously taking us with him.

But it doesn't have to be this way. There are several biblical principles we can use in working with and following other Christians. By applying these principles, we can survive the fall of a leader.

First, beware. Recognize what Jesus, Paul, Peter, and John warned us about. There are charlatans, Christian leaders who look like the real thing but aren't. They may come to you wearing the mantle of a shepherd (who typically wore a coat made of wool) which inspires your confidence and commitment, but they're "ravenous wolves" (Matthew 7:15). That means they're out to devour the sheep. Their purpose is self-aggrandizement.

How do you spot such a person? Jesus said, "You'll know them by their fruits" (7:20). What do they build? A personal empire? Schools and ministries named after them? Mountains of wealth funneled in their direction.? Questionable accounting practices? Constant praise toward themselves? Self-exaltation? If so, you know very well they're not building Christ's kingdom. Like Paul said to Titus, "They profess to know God, but by their deeds they deny Him" (Titus 1:16).

If you want to know if a man (or woman) is a spiritual fraud, look at his deeds. What's he doing? What's he producing? Where is the focus of his ministry? Don't just hear his words. He can be a vibrant, dynamite speaker. In fact, they usually are. What matters are his actions, what he does with the ministry, Word, pulpit, and money he controls.

Second, leaders are sinners, too. No spiritual leader has a corner on the holiness market. They're sinners; they will sin. The issue is, do they live up to the qualities Scripture establishes as necessary for leaders? The characteristics are listed in I Timothy 3:1-7 and Titus 1:5-9. The traits listed by Paul and given by God are high, idealistic, and acutely moral. But they're not impossible. Millions of godly men and women who follow Christ live them daily. That doesn't mean they never make a mistake, nor that every moment of every day they live out those characteristics perfectly. No one is perfect. What matters is the pattern of their lives.

But the role of a leader is a sacred trust. That's why James said, "Let not many of you become teachers, my brethren, knowing that as such we shall incur a stricter judgment" (James 3:1). No one should seek to lead who's not willing to live a pure, God-honoring life before the Lord. That's the cost.

But while leaders are sinners, they should have learned to overcome their sins in the power and grace of Christ *to a high degree.* That means nearly all external sins and verbal sins have been brought under control for the most part. The last area is mental, the most difficult of all. Leaders walking with Christ and in His power should have reached a point in their maturity and growth where they've conquered many of these problems. If they haven't, how can they help others or govern the church?

Third, the biblical pattern for dealing with sinning leaders is confrontation. Samuel rebuked King Saul for sacrificing the burnt offering in the place of the priest (I Samuel 13:8-14), and the king lost his kingdom for his sons. When he failed to follow God's orders about the Amalekites (I Samuel 15), he received a death sentence. Nathan confronted David about Bathsheba and Uriah (II Samuel 12). John the Baptist confronted Herod about his adultery with his brother's wife

(Matthew 14:4). Paul reproved Peter in public for refusing to eat with the Gentiles (Galatians 2:11-21). He also exhorted Timothy to get on with his ministry (II Timothy 1:8–2:3).

The leaders in our midst who sin should be confronted. Privately. Directly. Gently. With an eye to restoration. If they continue in sin, the process of church discipline as given in Matthew 18:15-17 should be followed.

But that doesn't make it easy. I have had to confront men who strayed from biblical principles and sinned in their ministries. I found that simply working up the courage to speak with them took much prayer and seeking God's grace. I also discovered a deep grief and pain in my own heart that it came to that point. I didn't want to speak harshly with those people. I loved them and wanted only to see them find fulfillment and success in their ministries. These have been some of the most painful moments in my life.

With grief I have written letters pointing out major sins. On only one occasion have I received a personal, kind letter in return, accepting my reproof and thanking me for caring enough to confront.

Remember that the purpose of confrontation is restoration, not exposure, explusion, or excoriation. You want that person to return to a genuine walk with Jesus, not to be destroyed or ridiculed.

Fourth, pray. Leaders in Christ's church today are suffering an incredible onslaught from the powers of hell. They need our prayer support more than anything else.

We tend to be a little glib about that. Giving money and time are so much more concrete. . . and easier. But I think that's because we don't understand the real power of God. A leader with hordes of money and lots of workers can come to nothing. A man with few pray-ers can accomplish great things for the kingdom of God.

When Charles Spurgeon preached in the Metropolitan

Tabernacle, huge crowds listened to his potent messages. But every Sunday, in a small room underneath the pulpit, a group of men and women prayed even as he preached. He attributed his great powers to them and to the Lord they entreated, not himself.

The power of prayer is amply illustrated in a book about John Hyde, called *Praying Hyde,* by Francis A. McGraw. In it the author tells about the life of this committed prayer-maker. At one time during his mission in India, he prayed that he would lead one person to Christ a day. At the end of that year there were well over 365 new converts to Christ. The next year he prayed for two converts a day. Again, come the same season the following year, John Hyde had seen over 800 come to Jesus. He became bolder. "Four," he prayed, "four every day to Jesus." Sure enough, at the end of that long year over 1600 had come in faith. When he returned to England, Hyde underwent some tests for a heart condition. The doctor was astonished. He discovered a heart twisted completely out of its cavity. Hyde attributed it to his emotional, convicted prayer habits.

Pray for those who lead you. They may never know of your hours before the throne on their behalf. But God will know. And He works in response to our petitions.

8/DISQUALIFIED FROM YOUR EVENT

In the 1930s, Louisiana State University sported a monster heavyweight, six feet six inches tall, named C.D. "Bigboy" Blalock. He entered a match with a stocky fellow from Mississippi State. It wasn't even considered a worthy match; the other guy was obviously outclassed.

In the second round, Bigboy wheeled out with a devastating roundhouse. However, the Mississippi lad stepped forward and notched his head in Bigboy's arm at the elbow. With his head acting as a fulcrum, Bigboy's roundhouse whipped all the way around, catching himself with a solid whack on the chin. Bigboy staggered, flailed at the rope, meandered around the ring, then collapsed on the floor—out for the count. His is an ignominious fame: the only boxer in history who scored a knockout with a punch to his own jawbone.

Like Bigboy Blalock, Christians sometimes knock themselves out of service to the Lord. Paul's words in I Corinthians 9:26-27 should give us sober pause as we sprint ahead into new ministries and work. "Therefore I run in such a way, as not without aim; I box in such a way, as not beating the air; but I buffet my body and make it my slave, lest possibly, after I have preached to others, I myself should be disqualified."

Sober, heartrending words.

Disqualification. It can bring terrific disillusionment, especially for the Christian who sees God as sovereign, all powerful, wise, and good. The first question they often ask— those who have suffered defrockings, loss of a ministry, loss of the right to be an elder or a teacher in a church, loss of leadership—is, "How could you let me do that, Lord? Why didn't you stop me?"

There But For The Grace Of God

It's only by the grace of God that any of us survives our own sinful nature. Anyone who can sit on the sidelines and scoff at a man or woman of God who has fallen is fooling himself. "Therefore let him who thinks he stands take heed lest he fall" (I Corinthians 10:12). Our grip on ourselves, our ability to fend off sin comes only by God's grace and through His strength. Any of us can fall from leadership through sin. Even as I write, I can think of ten people whom I once revered, or at least considered important Christian leaders, who have fallen through public sin.

Biblical Sinners

The Bible overflows with saints, leaders, and others who fell through sin. Some of the more obvious ones are David's sin with Bathsheba and his subsequent murder of her husband, Uriah (II Samuel 11–12). Moses sinned by striking the rock when God had warned him only to speak to it (Numbers 20:1-13). Look at Samson's lustful affair with Delilah (Judges 16:1-30); King Saul's presumption in offering sacrifices without God's permission (I Samuel 13:1-14) and his partial obediences (I Samuel 15:1-31); Achan's thefts (Joshua 7:1-26); Peter's three denials about being Jesus' disciple (Mark 14:66-72), and Ananias and Sapphira's sin of false giving (Acts 5:1-11). All these people suffered devastating consequences from their sins.

Such sinning often leads to a strange form of disillusionment.

The Components of Disillusionment Through Sin

I see at least four elements to how we react when caught in a fault.

The first is *shame.* We don't want to see anyone, face anyone, answer to anyone about what has happened. There's a deep sense of embarrassment in the presence of others.

When I was in third grade, a friend and I bought a box of one hundred match packs. We played with them behind his house until his mother caught us. That evening, his father stopped by my house to talk with my father. Afterward, my Dad confronted me about it. I was terrified, and I made up a story about the neighbor boy and how he'd bought the matches for us. To my horror, my Dad said he'd have to talk to my friend's father. That night he went over to their house.

I went to bed, literally shaking in my pajamas. And rightly so. About ten o'clock I was awakened to the tune of six stripes with a yardstick. My father told me never to lie like that again or I'd receive worse.

I thought it was over until the next day. Then I had to face my friend, the one I'd lied about. Shame engulfed me. I didn't know what to say or do.

That's small pain compared to what we might go through as an adult, especially someone who has been active in a church. People have been known to flee into seclusion for months if not years as a result of their sin. They become completely disillusioned with themselves, with life, with God. And for what? A little romp? A few dollars more? A tall tale?

The second element is *blame.* When we find ourselves in such a circumstance, we usually seek to blame someone. It's a process of rationalization. Often we try to blame God Himself. "Why didn't you stop me? Why didn't you say something? How could you let me do such a thing?" We take such a high view of God's omnipotence that we actually expect Him to halt us in our defiance and sinful pattern of life.

As one who has always held a strong view of God's control over this world, I've found that it's a convenient step to blame

Him for anything I do wrong. Somehow our ideas about sovereignty fail to consider man's responsibility in the same breath. God warns us. He disciplines. At times He even engineers events to stop us. Other times, when we refuse to heed His warnings, we must suffer the consequences of our willfulness. Adam and Eve did. David did. John Mark did.

God wants us to obey Him because we love and revere Him not at a spiritual gunpoint. We cannot blame His sovereignty for our sinfulness. We are responsible.

The third response to such sin is *bitterness*. Once we've gotten beyond the shame and the blame, there's still reality to handle. Sooner or later, if the Spirit is working in us, we'll see ourselves as the real culprits. But instead of acting in true, godly repentance, too often we resort to bitterness, anger, and discouragement. We blame ourselves for our own crimes to the point that we destroy ourselves emotionally. We may even try to manipulate God. We go on and on, telling God how poorly He must think of us.

But this isn't a repentant response to personal sin; it is rank manipulation. We try to make God feel bad. But what we need to do is simply repent and decide not to resort to sinful means of solving our problems.

The fourth component of this kind of disillusionment is *hopelessness*. Sometimes we reach the point where we feel we've been disqualified forever. One of the ways we show this is to weep and say, "How can you ever forgive me?" And then conclude that they can't forgive. Not people. Not the family. Not God.

But all this is disillusionment. It's not real. It's not the truth. It's not what God's Word says.

Hope Extended

What, then, does the Bible say about such sin? I believe we, in the twentieth century, need to gain a new sobriety about sin. Sin is serious. It quenches the Spirit. It grieves God. It destroys relationships. It can never be undone. We can't go back and rearrange history. When we sin, we set in motion forces that will affect life up until death or the return of Christ. It's irrevocable.

What, then, does Scripture say to us about such sin?

Our Responsibility

The first thing we must reckon with is *our responsibility before God.*

God has created us as free agents. We choose to act in certain ways. Never are we *forced* to choose what we know is sin. Rather, when we sin, we usually know it's sin, but we choose it anyway. Our responsibility before God says that we are personally accountable for all our actions (Romans 14:10-12). We always have a choice: To obey the truth, or to disobey God.

But what about God's sovereignty over such sin? Couldn't He stop us if He wanted?

Certainly. But God has created a world in which He is in absolute, sovereign control over every event, thought, and word that happens, yet at the same time allows each of us free choices. God is in control, but He does not force us to do anything we don't consciously choose and want to do.

"But that's a contradiction!"

No, not at all. The truth is that God is in charge, and we are responsible for our actions. I'm not a robot. And He's not a dictator. He has actually blended His sovereignty and our responsibility in such a way that they work in perfect harmony.

For instance, the death of Christ. Look at Acts 4:27-28. There, the disciples prayed to God, saying that all of Jerusalem gathered against Jesus—Herod, Pontius Pilate, the Gentiles, and the people of Israel—to do "whatever Thy hand

and Thy purpose predestined to occur." In other words, God planned that it would all happen, from the beginning.

Who was responsible for the sin? Look at Peter in Acts 5:30 speaking to the Council. "The God of our fathers raised up Jesus, whom you had put to death by hanging Him on a cross." Earlier, in Acts 2:36, he concluded his Pentecost message with the words, "Therefore let all the house of Israel know for certain that God has made Him both Lord and Christ—this Jesus whom you crucified."

Clearly, God says that He planned and predestinated the crucifixion of Jesus, yet He places the responsibility for this act of murder on others. How can it be?

In His omniscience, God knew precisely what everyone would do. He sovereignly stayed in charge so that, ultimately, His plan for the redemption of man would be accomplished. He could only do it through Jesus Christ taking the death penalty in our place. He also knew precisely how everyone would treat Jesus if He sent Him to live on earth to preach and teach. He knew they'd kill Him because they would hate Him and the message of a personal accountability for sin. God worked within that framework, and His plan was accomplished.

God did not force anyone to do anything. They simply did what their sinful natures made them want to do.

God was not unfair or insidious. He simply sent His Son to tell people the truth. They decided to crucify Him. His plan allowed that crucifixion to act as the redemption point of mankind.

The point is that you and I are responsible for our sin. If we choose to commit a terrible sin, we choose to do so consciously and without coercion, even though God is sovereign. We can't blame Him. The only one we can blame is ourselves.

The Totality of Forgiveness

The second thing we need to understand is *the totality of God's forgiveness*. Scripture gives us a graphic picture of how God forgives. In Micah 7:19 He says it's buried in the depths of the sea. In Isaiah 38:17, the prophet says God has put them behind His back. In Isaiah 44:22, God reminds us He has wiped them out. In Isaiah 43:25, He tells us He doesn't remember them anymore. And in Psalm 103:12, we are told that God has removed them from us as far as the east is from the west.

God's forgiveness is total. He'll never bring our failures up in heaven or eternity. When we sin, and ask for forgiveness, God forgives. "There is forgiveness with Thee, that Thou mayest be feared" (Psalm 130:4). It's a complete, forgetful, hiding-them-away-forever forgiveness. "If we confess our sins, He is faithful and righteous to forgive us our sins and to cleanse us from all unrighteousness" (I John 1:9).

Clara Barton, founder of the Red Cross, was once reminded of a cruel act someone had done to her. She replied that she didn't remember it. The person went into more detail, astonished that she could forget such a thing. Clara responded, "I distinctly remember forgetting that one."

That's godly forgiveness. Any Christian who has sinned can know that, like the prodigal son, God's only response to repentance is to slay the fatted calf, put a ring on our finger and a robe on our back, and to declare a feast in our honor. He longs for fellowship, not prison visitation.

The Reality of Consequences

Still, we can't take advantage of such truth. There's another equally sobering fact to consider: *when we sin, there are consequences*. When Moses struck the rock in defiance of God's command, he lost the right to go into the land of milk and honey with the rest of the people (Numbers 20). When David sinned with Bathsheba, God said He'd repay him four times for his sin (II Samuel 12). When Martha busied herself in the kitchen, she lost out on the Lord's teaching and earned His rebuke (Luke 10:38-42).

This sobering fact stands out above all others when it comes to sin. Even though God forgives, there are consequences to sin which He will not override.

One of the first questions Christians in the public eye usually ask when they have been confronted with gross sin is: "When can I get back into my ministry?" Unfortunately, that's not repentance. That's not godly submission to Christ. One has to wonder if they understand what it means to walk with Jesus. They show no concern for their failure. Their response is selfish rather than humble. All they seem to care about is, "How will this affect my right to a public forum, money, and admirers?" Such people show that they have even less of a right to pursue their public ministries.

If we sin willfully, we must recognize that there are consequences. When Nadab and Abihu sinned by offering strange fire before the Lord, they were killed instantly (Leviticus 10:1-2). Achan and his whole family were stoned following his confession of sin (Joshua 7). The question we need to ask is not, "Why did God do this to them?" but, "Why doesn't He do it to us?" Too often we count on God's grace and overlook His justice. In fact, we sometimes barter with His grace at our own peril. We go into sin with our eyes open, thinking, "Oh, He'll forgive me afterward," when we should recognize this might be the time He chooses to strike us dead!

The Possibility of Disqualification

Earlier, we noted a reality Paul mentioned in I Corinthians 9:27, his fear that he could be disqualified. This is a fourth element of the scriptural response to personal sin: *the possiblity of disqualification.*

Let's ask several questions. First, what is it? Second, what sins constitute grounds for it? Third, can anyone ever overcome it?

1. *What is it?*

The word Paul uses is *adokimos,* which means "unfit, unqualified, not standing the test, worthless." In most instances in the New Testament, it speaks of someone who is summarily rejected and dismissed as a disciple or minister of Christ (Romans 1:28, II Corinthians 13:5-7, II Timothy 3:8-9, Titus 1:16). In one passage, ground is rejected because it doesn't produce fruit (Hebrews 6:7-8).

In I Corinthians 9:24-27, Paul uses an example from athletics. An athlete could run the race, participate in the whole event, and then suffer total disqualification because he did not "compete according to the rules" (II Timothy 2:5). The world saw this happen during the 1988 Olympics in Seoul, Korea. Ben Johnson set a world record and beat his opponents by several strides. But he lost his gold medal because it was proven he had used steriods—a banned drug—to win over opponents who had followed the rules. He was disqualified.

In our day, a large number of ministers and people in the public eye have experienced this problem. They commit a sin (or sins); it's found out, and they lose their position. For a period of time, and in some cases for the rest of their lives, they are barred from public ministry and leadership.

Several prominent first-century Christians experienced this. Peter denied Jesus three times, but later repented and returned to service as a pillar of godliness (John 18:15-27; 21:3-17, Acts 1:15—2:41). In another instance, he fell to peer pressure and legalism and was rebuked by Paul in public (Galatians 2:14-21). Demas left Paul in the middle of his work and went to Thessalonica (II Timothy 4:10). Paul added that he "loved this present world." Timothy himself suffered from personal timidity about preaching the Word (II Timothy 1:8-12), Phygelus and Hermogenes deserted Paul in Asia (II Timothy 1:15). Hymenaeus and Philetus taught heresy (II Timothy 2:17-18). Paul even delivered several over to Satan for personal discipline (Hymenaeus and Alexander—I Timothy 1:20; the man who committed sexual sin with his father's wife—I Corinthians 5:1-5). John Mark deserted Paul during the first missionary journey (Acts 15:36-40), but later Paul called him "profitable to me for the ministry" (II Timothy 4:11).

2. *What sins could disqualify one?*

Paul outlines the qualities a pastor or a deacon should possess if they aspire to these offices. They're found in I Timothy 3:1-13 and Titus 1:5-9. He makes it clear that such leaders are to "be" these things. They're not just character traits one aspires to have. Anyone can do that. No. Rather, they're traits a person is characterized *by*. They're what this person is.

What are they? From I Timothy 3:1-7, they are:

Above reproach	Not pugnacious
The husband of one wife	Gentle
(a one-woman man)	Uncontentious
Temperate	Free from the love of
Prudent	money
Respectable	One who manages his own
Hospitable	household well (control-
Able to teach	ling children with
Not addicted to wine	dignity)
	Not a new convert

Titus adds a few more:

Having children who	Sensible
believe	Just

Not accused of	Devout
dissipation or rebellion	Self-controlled
Not self-willed	Holding fast the faithful
Not quick-tempered	word—discerning sound
Loving what is good	doctrine

Any elder who fails to live up to these characteristics is to be disciplined. A charge must be brought by at least two witnesses (I Timothy 5:19). If an elder continues in his sin (that is, he doesn't repent privately before the others involved), he is to be rebuked publicly (I Timothy 5:20).

What, then, totally disqualifies someone from ministry? In I Corinthians 6:9-10, Galatians 5:19-21, Romans 1:18-32, and II Timothy 3:1-9 Paul lists sins which, if they lead to condemnation for non-Christians, must be certain disqualifiers for those in Christian leadership.

Sin is, in the eyes of God, most serious in leaders. Solomon lost his kingdom because he worshipped idols and turned away from the Lord (I Kings 11:1-11). Does that seem rather harsh? Yes, but when you're dealing with people who set the standards for millions of others, then you're dealing with extremely serious business. God cannot allow His kingdom to be led by people who live in sin.

Does that mean leaders must be perfect? By no means. But some things are so serious, a person renders himself disqualified.

That brings us to the third question: *Can it ever be overcome?*

Frankly, I don't know. Scripture is silent on the issue. It's obvious that Peter, John Mark, and Timothy were restored to service. Others, like Moses and King Saul, lost all rights to leadership and service. For some, Demas, Hymenaeus, Alexander, Philetus, it's not clear what happened. But whatever happens, there is always hope. God is the God of grace, mercy, and forgiveness.

But the issue before us is the disillusionment we feel—even as "ordinary" Christians—as a result of such a fall. We must remember that if we have suffered disqualification, only godly, committed pursuit of the principles of Scripture will overcome our disillusionment with ourselves and our sense of failure.

The Security of God's Sovereignty

But there's a last principle any disillusioned person must note: *there is security in God's sovereignty.* Remember Romans 8:28? God can override any sin, any mishap, any evil, and bring good out of that circumstance. He truly is in charge. If we fall, God knew that fall would happen, and we can be sure that if we repent, follow Him, and walk closely with Him again, that He will bless our lives. The thing to avoid is letting our disillusionment drive us further away from Him.

As I write, I am aware of a man in the midst of a difficult situation. For several years now he has been out of the pastoral ministry because of a situation that led to his resignation in a previous pastorate. Only in the last year has he felt the confidence and security of getting back into the ministry. Yet, just as he began to pursue this and as churches responded, a situation arose in his home which made it impossible for him to return to a church ministry. He said it was sheer agony calling various churches and withdrawing his application.

I don't think he has been disqualified. But one thing is sure: If God wants him in the pastorate again or to function as an elder, He will enable him to overcome his problems and obtain the qualifications necessary. I have confidence that this setback is not a setdown. It's not permanent.

That gives us hope. Our Lord is in the business of redemption not revenge, restoration not ruin. "I know the plans that I have for you," He declares, "plans for welfare and not for calamity to give you a future and a hope" (Jeremiah 29:11).

That's our Lord.

No more disillusionment, then. Rather, pursue determination, perseverance, endurance, discipline. Those are the elements of hope, of heaven, of holiness.

PART II: CAUSES

*An examination of the role and relationship
of expectations.*

9/You Can't, If You Think You Can't

I'm convinced the primary cause of disillusionment, discouragement, and disappointment in life is faulty expectations.

Think about it.

• Doug becomes a Christian during his junior summer in college. He can't wait to get back to the campus. He's convinced God will convert everyone—his fraternity brothers, those agnostic professors, his roommate. But when he returns, he finds his roommate has already heard it all; he's not interested. His fraternity brothers avoid him because he'll no longer indulge in their drinking sprees and drugs. And his professors knock so many holes in his arguments, he's not sure what he believes.

In total discouragement he trudges to his room after that first week and kneels by his bed to pray, "Lord, I just don't understand. I thought you could do anything. I feel like my faith is shattered."

• Chuck marries his college sweetheart, and they spin off

into the wild blue. Two years down the road, they have their first child. Two years more and it's number two. But problems have crept in those last months. The arguments were so furious, Ellen slapped him—twice. Then, just last week, six years into their marriage, Chuck lost control. He punched his wife in the stomach right in front of the kids. Moments later, he was weeping. "What has happened to us? We're Christians, aren't we?" He can't even hold his head up anymore. He feels as though he slinks around everywhere, unable even to smile. "What has gone wrong?" he wonders. "Why doesn't God do something?"

• A leader in the church leads John to Christ. John becomes a zealous disciple. Then one day he learns his friend has committed adultery; he's leaving the church. John doesn't understand and goes home deeply depressed.

These folks had certain expectations about life.

Doug believed God was so great and mighty that He'd start a revival on his campus—and use him to do it.

Chuck was convinced that Christian marriages should live far above the problems of the common couple.

John had the idea that certain Christians don't sin.

But none of these expectations are true. In fact, each conflicts with specific statements of Scripture. God has not promised anywhere that everything will go right in life just because we are Christians. In fact, He's made it clear that things *won't* be that way (II Timothy 3:12; Matthew 10:16-18,24-36). Life will go wrong. Problems will occur.

Furthermore, God has never promised that we will have success, prosperity, health, or happiness the way the world defines these things. Rather, He's warned us that we will be treated as outcasts and rejects (Matthew 10; John 15:18; John 17:14; I John 3:10-13). Our lives and work may count for nothing in the eyes of the world.

Finally, God never said that He will automatically draw people to Himself just because we pray. We must go, sow, and hoe the soil, trusting Him to produce the results. But there's no guarantee (Matthew 18:18-23; John 6:44; I Corinthians 3:6-8).

The Idea Persists

Nonetheless, the idea persists. Most Christians know that God doesn't promise a problem-free existence on Planet Earth. But for some reason, they think they'll be an exception.

It's funny. All my Christian life I've known that God doesn't promise health, wealth, and happiness. Yet, deep down I think that someday I'll write a best-selling book that will make me rich. I have all these tremendous plans. First, make a million dollars. Next, support ten missionaries. Finally, live off what's left. I can think of all these people I'd like to bless financially—good people, committed people, people who don't receive much materially.

But is that the way God operates? What if, instead, He has decided that it's much better for me to learn to live by faith day-by-day than to make a million and help others not to have to live by faith ever again?

And, why should I think health will always abide with me? Or that I would make the best-seller list?

I don't know. But something within me argues with God's Word and wants to believe I'm an exception to the rule!

This is something I'm convinced we all do. If you don't think so, then why do you ever get angry about anything? Most of our anger occurs because we feel neglected, overlooked, cheated, or that our rights are being trampled on. If we agree we have no rights (as Scripture indicates— Galatians 5:12-15; James 4:1-12; I Peter 4:12-19), then what's there to yell about?

Have you ever thought, "Why me, Lord?" What is that if not the cry that says, "I should be an exception"?

This is part of the source of our false expectations. We know the truth, but we don't want to believe the truth. We think God will cause us to rise above the normal even to the point of overruling scriptural principles.

Three Basic Areas of Expectation

There are three basic areas in which people have expectations.

About Self   *About Others*   *About God*

When it comes down to ground zero, all of our expectations relate to something we expect of someone—whether it's ourselves, others, or God Himself. And in each of these cases we have examples in Scripture, as well as life today, where people expected something of someone and that someone didn't fulfill their expectations. Let's look at the problem of expectations of yourself.

Oh, Those High Expectations

What is it we often expect of ourselves that leads to trouble? Try these:

- That you will usually (if not always) succeed.
- While the job may be difficult for others, you're sure you'll know what to do.
- That you won't make any serious mistakes.
- That you would never commit gross sin.
- That you could never fail in the important things in life—your marriage, your job, your schooling, your parenting.

- While others might die young, you'll live to rip-roaring old age.
- While others might get the disease, it'll certainly pass you by.
- That you're truly likable.
- That you'll automatically be rewarded for doing good.
- That people just naturally get along with you and want to be your friend.

What others might you add to the list? There are hundreds of little expectations we place on ourselves moment by moment which can lead to disillusionment if we haven't placed them on line with truth.

A young man told me that all his life people assured him he had what it took to make it big in this world. He moved out into his first few jobs with high expectations of success. But it wasn't so fast in coming. He enrolled in an MBA program and soon discovered that while others seemed to digest statistics and business principles easily, he struggled. One day he said to me that it had been a difficult climb, but he had finally come to realize he was, "just an average guy, not destined for greatness." It stunned him at first. It was inconceivable. But as he learned to accept his weak points, he realized great freedom and renewed joy.

Peter: The Problem of Me, Myself and I

The one person besides Jesus who takes up more space in the Gospels than any other is Simon Peter. Jesus renamed Simon and gave him the name Peter, or "little rock." It became his trademark. Peter rocked his generation awake. Christ used him as the church's primary foundation stone. His letters in Scripture offer solid counsel to those on the edge of the cliff. He was the one who jumped out of the boat to walk on water with Jesus (Matthew 14:29). When Jesus asked who men said

He was, Peter didn't hesitate. "Thou art the Christ, the Son of the Living God" (Matthew 16:16). It was Peter who was on the mountain when Jesus was transfigured (Matthew 17:1-8). He was part of the inner circle of three. He possessed boldness, eloquence, insight, determination.

He also had weaknesses. One of them, apparently, was a distinct lack of self-understanding and self-control. He rarely thought out his actions. And it got him into trouble—frequently.

When Jesus rebuked him with the words, "Get behind Me, Satan! You are a stumbling block to Me; for you are not setting your mind on God's interests, but man's" (Matthew 16:23), they were Jesus' harshest rebuke to anyone ever. Even the Pharisees were only sons of their father, the devil (John 6:44).

It must have taken a terrific toll on the man. Though nothing in Scripture indicates Peter's response, every time we see him thereafter, he's trying to prove something.

The Most Potent Example

Yet, Scripture's most potent example of disillusionment through wrong expectations comes from Peter's denial of Jesus. Jesus warned him in Luke 22:31-34 that he was in terrific danger. Satan had requested to "sift him like wheat." But Peter not only refused to accept the Lord's words (an incredible act of unbelief), but to argue and insist he would never do such a thing.

What was the problem? Peter simply couldn't imagine it happening. He considered himself the most committed of the disciples. Therefore he expected to remain loyal to Jesus no matter what provocation came his way. Moreover, Jesus had said He would build His church on Peter. That was enough. Peter could never deny Jesus—he was too important! But most of all, he figured not even Satan himself could lead him astray. He'd outfox the fox. He thought he could handle anything. He was above failure—in his own mind.

All these expectations worked against Peter.

- They made him reject God's Word.
- They caused him to underestimate Satan.
- They led him to remain unprepared.
- They appealed to his pride.
- They led him to use poor judgment.

And he fell.

Getting Yourself in Focus

What expectations do you have of yourself that are leading you to make foolish decisions or to use poor judgment? Are you making yourself out to be more than you are? If so, you may be setting yourself up for a big knockdown.

How, then, do we avoid falling prey to wrong expectations of ourselves? Only one way: through honest and humble self-appraisal. Humility is not a low opinion of yourself; it's a right opinion—God's opinion. What is that opinion? I see at least five scriptural elements.

1. *I am fallen* (Romans 3:10).

Therefore you will struggle with sin and self. Expect to struggle, to fall, and to get up and struggle again. It never ends so long as you live on this planet.

Paul spoke of this struggle in Romans 7. In verse 15, he begins the litany of the depraved man. "For that which I am doing, I do not understand; for I am not practicing what I would like to do, but I am doing the very thing I hate." What a contradiction! He couldn't understand it at all.

From this we see a principle: evil is inside us (7:21). It's at the very heart of our being, like a vine that has wrapped itself around the wall of our hearts, reaching into every crevice and cranny.

"What a wretched man I am!" cries Paul. "Who will set me

free from this body which does nothing but work evil?"

He comes up with the answer in verse 25: "Thanks be to God through Jesus Christ our Lord!"

Only in Christ can our fallenness be overcome. How? Through Christ entering and permeating every element of our hearts, minds, souls, bodies. Through His influence on our thoughts, emotions, and actions. Through the indwelling presence of the Holy Spirit who goes with us wherever we are.

But we have to begin with our fallenness. It's our fallenness that makes us expect the wrong things of ourselves. Only in Christ can we get the perspective that sees as He sees and does as He does.

2. *I am weak.*

Jesus said, "Apart from Me you can do nothing" (John 15:5). Don't fall into the trap of acting without praying, giving advice without consulting His Word, offering a hand to help before you've offered your life to Christ. You are totally dependent on Christ's power, plan, and purpose.

We tend to subvert this in our minds. "I'm my own man." "I can be anything I want to be." "I can do anything I set my mind to." These are expressions that rip against the grain of everything Scripture teaches. In reality, we are weak, dependent, incapable creatures apart from Christ.

Don't get me wrong. People without Christ can do plenty as far as this world is concerned. Make money. Wage war. Win a heavyweight bout. Be awarded the Nobel Prize. Run a race. Whack out a homerun.

But those are really trivialities. When it comes to pleasing God, doing good in His sight, accomplishing something for the kingdom of God, we are impotent. Everything we do is tainted, without lasting value in the eyes of God. Anything not done in faith through dependence on Christ is a waste.

When D. L. Moody conducted evangelistic crusades in

England in the late 1800s, the British press watched him closely. Many were astounded at the crowds that came to hear him preach. One reporter wrote, "Mr. Moody butchers the King's English. He has a nasal tone. He has an unpleasant, high-pitched voice. He is overweight and generally rough in appearance. I see nothing in Mr. Moody to account for his marvelous success."

Moody replied when he read the clipping. "That's the secret. There is nothing *in me* to account for it."

Like the Lord told Paul, "My grace is sufficient for you, for power is perfected in weakness" (II Corinthians 12:9).

3. *I am part of a great plan.*

"I know the plans that I have for you," God told His people (Jeremiah 29:11). It's as true for us today as it was during the Babylonian exile. It's also exciting to know that we fit into His vast eternal plan, and it's humbling to realize we're a small part of a big picture. Your life, personality, talents, and abilities were all endowed with a purpose. God has placed you where you are and made you what you are as part of something far bigger.

For that reason, we can expect God to use us as He pleases, not as we please. He has plans for us, yes, but they're *His* plans, not necessarily ours.

What is God's plan, His will? The study of the word "will" in the Bible is a fascinating one for anyone who truly wants to know God's will. Here are just a few verses.

The conclusion, when all has been heard, is: fear God and keep His commandments, because this applies to every person. (Ecclesiastes 12:13)

"Teacher, which is the great commandment in the Law?" And He said to him, "You shall love the Lord your God with all your heart, and with all your soul, and with all your mind." (Matthew 22:36-37)

I urge you therefore, brethren, by the mercies of God, to present your bodies a living and holy sacrifice, acceptable to God, which is your spiritual service of worship. And do not be conformed to this world, but be transformed by the renewing of your mind, that you may prove what the will of God is, that which is good and acceptable and perfect.
(Romans 12:1-2)

And from the throne of Heaven:
"Worthy art Thou, our Lord and our God, to receive glory and honor and power, for Thou didst create all things, and because of Thy will they existed, and were created."
(Revelation 4:11)

We are part of a plan—a magnificent, masterful, monumental, all-encompassing plan—that God in His wisdom fabricated before you and I ever existed. God designed the plan for the purpose of glory—for Himself first, and also for His creation. When we see ourselves as part of His plan, we can relax and walk in the paths He's laid before us. Without fear. Without hesitation. Without complaint.

4. *I am gifted.*

God has given us specific gifts to use for Him in the church and in life. But beware of thinking you have certain gifts when you don't. Squirrels climb trees with the best, but they don't swim. Ducks make waves, but not up in treetops. Be clear about what gifts God has given you and use them, not the ones you wish you had.

I once read that Spurgeon said that if God gave an angel the job of sweeping the streets of London, he would do it with all the joy, skill, and excellence he could muster. What would matter to that angel was not the size of the job or its importance in the eyes of men, but God's importance in the eyes of all.

5. *I am highly valued.*

"I have loved you with an everlasting love," God said to Jeremiah (Jeremiah 31:3). Jesus demonstrated that love by dying for our sins (Romans 5:8). In effect, each Christian has the same value placed upon himself: the whole life and person of Jesus Christ. How "valuable" is Jesus? There can be no calculation.

We know this intrinsically. When we see dead animals on the side of the road, there may be little to no shock registered. But when the newspaper reports a baby found dead in a dumpster, it makes headlines. Why? Because something within us knows the value of a human life. It's inestimable. We're made in the image of God. No animal possesses that likeness.

Nonetheless, beyond this is the price of redemption. Jesus paid for every soul with His own blood, His own life. As Peter said, "You were not redeemed with perishable things like silver or gold from your futile way of life inherited from your forefathers, but with precious blood, as of a lamb unblemished and spotless, the blood of Christ" (I Peter 1:18-19).

How do you calculate the net worth of God? It's an impossibility. The only word we have for it is *infinite.*

And through the Lord Jesus Christ, God has placed an infinite value on every person who calls himself a child of God. That's how much He values us. But it is only by faith that we obtain infinite value in His eyes. Without faith, all our "righteous deeds are like a filthy garment" (Isaiah 64:6).

Years ago, I visited a pastor's office. As I waited to see him, a woman came in and sat down. We began to talk. She told me she was seeing the pastor for counseling and began telling me her problem with self-image. Then she told me that she'd read in the Bible that she was "fearfully and wonderfully made." Looking me squarely in the eye she said, "One thing I tell myself every day now is this: God doesn't make junk."

Indeed, God doesn't make junk. We're each His special creation.

Do You Have It?

As we fix these truths in our minds, we begin to get a picture. As we gain a godly perspective of ourselves, we bring our expectations into line. Then we see that yes, we do sin and make mistakes. If we fail to walk closely with the Lord, He may allow us to sin horribly. But we can repent and receive forgiveness. In Christ we can achieve reconciliation through humble admission of our own guilt. As we came back into line with God's plan, things begin to mesh together again.

10/DON'T PUT YOUR TRUST IN PRINCES

Expectations don't stop with self. We also have numerous expectations toward others. What are they?

- That others should do what we ask them to do... immediately, unquestioningly.
- That others should respect our rights and personhood.
- That others should give us the benefit of the doubt (as we will undoubtedly give them the same thing).
- That others should be kind.
- That others shouldn't mess things up.
- That others should recognize we're basically decent, kind, and loving.
- That others should be prompt in paying their bills (those owed to me, anyway).
- That others should do things right—the first time.

These kinds of expectations of others can grate on your psyche when they go unfulfilled. Many times throughout Scripture, leaders and saints suffered discouragement, depression, and disillusionment because of such expectations in the face of human failure and human nature. People—even Christians—suffer wrong at the hands of others.

David and King Saul

King Saul treated David about as poorly as one can treat another. The king was jealous, angry, vengeful, and unrelenting in his pursuit of David. He sought to kill the young man repeatedly.

Yet, David not only remained loyal to the king, he refused to compromise his principles even in the face of several perfect opportunities for revenge. When Saul came into the cave and then fell asleep (I Samuel 24:1-7), David's men encouraged him to kill the king, even suggesting God had given him this chance. But David refused, and only cut off a piece of Saul's robe. Then even that sin overwhelmed him with guilt and he said, "Far be it from me because of the Lord that I should do this thing to my lord, the Lord's anointed, to stretch out my hand against him . . . " (I Samuel 24:6).

What was it that kept David from doing wrong even in the face of the worst provocation? God's Word. "Do not touch my anointed ones" (I Chronicles 16:22). Certainly David expected better things of Saul. He probably envisioned serving in the king's court until Saul died of a ripe old age, and then he would become king. But those expectations dissolved in the poison of Saul's anger. David chose to do right even though he had been wronged and his hopes had disintegrated. His expectations didn't lead him into disillusionment.

Peter and John

Peter and the apostles are additional examples. In Acts 5:15-42, after healing the sick, they were both cast into prison. God released them through an angel, and the apostles went on preaching repentance and faith in Christ. When the Sanhedrin learned of their actions, they were dragged in under guard. When questioned and commanded to stop preaching Jesus, Peter took the opportunity and began preaching a sermon to the Sanhedrin. Talk about boldness! His words so convicted them that Luke says they "were cut to the quick" (Acts 5:33). They wanted the men executed. Gamaliel, however, a leading Pharisee, prevented them. So they decided to flog them and order them to speak no more in Christ's name. Then, they were released.

Flogging in those days was brutal. Ordinarily, a special group of soldiers were brought in to administer the punishment, experts in exacting the greatest pain from the victim.

What was the apostles' response after the punishment was given? Read Acts 5:41. "So they went on their way from the presence of the Council, rejoicing that they had been considered worthy to suffer shame for His name."

That's a remarkable response to evil. Too often I have found myself recoiling in anger at the slightest irritations. But these men rejoiced that God considered them worthy to suffer a horrible, undeserved beating. They were true biblicists. They took to heart Jesus' words in Matthew 5:11-12, "Blessed are you when men revile you, and persecute you, and say all kinds of evil against you falsely, on account of Me. Rejoice, and be glad, for your reward in heaven is great, for so they persecuted the prophets who were before you."

The apostles could have expected to be treated better. They might have complained about the persecution, or remarked that "only scoundrels act like that." But they didn't. Instead, they understood with a godly perspective the problems of living in a world populated by sinners.

King Saul and Samuel

Another interesting case occurs in I Samuel 13. King Saul assembled his army to fight the Philistines. Before he could fight, though, he was ordered by Samuel to wait until the prophet could arrive to make the burnt offerings. Samuel told him that he'd be there within seven days (I Samuel 10:8). The burnt offerings and peace offerings for Israel were critical; they insured that God was with them and ready to do battle.

Well, seven days passed. Meanwhile, Saul's army dwindled. People left in fear and aggravation, unwilling to wait so long for things to start. Saul became afraid and took matters into his own hands. He decided to offer the sacrifices himself. But the king had no right to do this. He was neither a priest nor a judge. Samuel wasn't even late. He'd already said he wouldn't be there for seven days. But Saul was afraid of losing all his men.

In a sense, King Saul felt "let down" by Samuel. He felt as though Samuel hadn't done his part, or, at least, should have come earlier before so many left. In this case, though, King Saul wrongly expected certain things to happen. His expectations were entirely sinful and self-willed.

It Can Make for a Difficult World

All this can make life supremely difficult. What makes all this worse is that we tend to have such high expectations of each other. Too often we expect that the other guy—
- should live up to biblical principles, even if we don't.
- should be kind and loving, even if we aren't.
- should understand, even when we're not understanding.
- should give me the benefit of the doubt, even if I don't give it to him.

But isn't that what we all do? Don't we (consciously or unconsciously) have high expectations of everyone else, and at the same time think that they should recognize our weaknesses and problems that excuse us from having to live up to those same expectations? How can we do that? It's the same issue Jesus pointed out in Matthew 7:1-4, "Why do you look at the speck in your brother's eye, but do not notice the log that is in your own eye?" We tend to excuse ourselves, while requiring the highest standards of everyone else.

It Doesn't Have To Be this Way

But it doesn't have to stay like this. What biblical principles apply to the problem of expectations of others?

Remember, *people will inevitably let you down.* They're sinners, and sinners sin.

Expect it. They'll fail to do what you asked oh, so specifically and nicely. They'll make excuses. They'll lie about what they did. They'll cover it up. Expect it. If you go around thinking so and so has no right to do such and such to you, and how could he/she, you'll soon be disillusioned.

TIME Magazine (12-17-79) reported a commotion that occurred on an Eastern Air Lines shuttle from Washington, D.C. bound for New York City. Apparently, several non-smokers became enraged when several smokers lit up. There was screaming, yelling, and every sort of insult you can imagine. Then the captain came on the intercom. He said, "Please act like adults. If this insurrection doesn't stop, I'm going to put this plane down."

It didn't stop. The captain put the plane down at Baltimore-Washington International Airport. A number of passengers canceled out. Others took another flight and made it to New York, three hours late. One disgusted commuter remarked, "I haven't seen a display like that since kindergarten."

That's the stuff of which wars are made. Yet, that's humanity.

Second, sometimes people will wrong you.

As Christians, we need to recognize that people will cheat, lie, and protect themselves. Some will be "out to get us." They'll do their worst to destroy us. Paul said, "Indeed, all who desire to live godly in Christ Jesus will be persecuted" (II Timothy 3:12). John said, "Do not marvel, brethren, if the world hates you" (I John 3:13). Peter said, "Do not be surprised at the fiery ordeal among you, which comes upon you for your testing, as though some strange thing were happening to you" (I Peter 4:12).

Third, people in whom you've put the greatest trust will sometimes harm you.

Even Jesus got that treatment. In Psalm 41:9, David prophesies of the betrayal of Jesus by Judas Iscariot. He said, "Even my close friend, in whom I trusted, who ate my bread, has lifted up his heel against me." John 13:18-27 is the fulfillment of that prophecy. Judas had the trust of the other disciples; he carried their money. Even though Jesus knew from the start that he would betray Him, He repeatedly gave Judas every opportunity to enter the kingdom.

Don't trust people blindly. That probably sounds like a wretched way to view the world, but it's scriptural. In Psalm 146:3, the Psalmist writes, "Do not trust in princes, in mortal man, in whom there is no salvation." Whom to trust then? God. "How blessed is he whose help is the God of Jacob, whose hope is in the Lord his God; who made heaven and earth, the sea and all that is in them; who keeps faith forever; who executes justice for the oppressed; who gives food to the hungry. The Lord sets the prisoners free" (146:5-7).

This doesn't mean you shouldn't have a trusting spirit toward most of the people you meet. But we all need to carry a realization that people are sinners, and they will not act according to our expectations or necessarily in our best interests. Jesus knew this. After His first Passover in Jerusalem, many people saw Jesus' miracles and believed in Him. But Jesus didn't rejoice. John writes, "But Jesus, on His part, was not entrusting Himself to them, for He knew all men . . . for he Himself knew what was in man" (John 2:24-25). Jesus knew that many of those very people who "believed" in Him would one day scream for His crucifixion.

Neither does this mean that we should go through life virtually paranoid. By God's grace He does deliver us both from our enemies and from our friends. We can trust people in most of the normal transactions of life. It's the extraordinary ones that get us.

How Do You Survive?

What's the balance then? How do you avoid disillusionment with people? Have biblical expectations. Expect people to let you down, sin, hurt you, even malign you. Don't look on it as the final straw or a fate worse than death. It happens to all of us. It's part of living in a sinful world. Just be prepared with a Christlike attitude, "Because the foolishness of God is wiser than men, and the weakness of God is stronger than men" (I Corinthians 1:25). Memorize Proverbs 3:5-6 and study Colossians 3:1-17.

Expecting the worst isn't exactly the best procedure for living disillusionment-free in this world of ours, and if you always expect the best, you won't be discouraged. But if you demand the best and settle only for perfection, disillusionment will color your life—1440 minutes a day.

11/Is Your God The True God?

We don't have expectations just of ourselves and others. Some of our highest and greatest expectations involve God Himself. When He doesn't do what we think He should, we can become deeply despondent.

I remember finding out about the doctrine of predestination as a young Christian. At the time I was working with a group of young people and seminarians from a strongly Calvinistic background. Every other word they uttered, it seemed to me, related to predestination and God's sovereignty.

When they first confronted me with it, I fought boldly against it. Each day I'd find some new passage that supported such things as free will and God's love for all the world. But they'd always push me back to Romans 9, Ephesians 1, and other passages. I couldn't get around those potent words in Romans 9:13, "Jacob have I loved, but Esau have I hated." And Matthew 22:14, "For many are called, but few are chosen." They so emphasized God's sovereign election, I became nearly distraught. What was worse was that I seemed to be finding it everywhere I looked in Scripture.

I remember the climax of that time. One day I went out on the beach, laid out my blanket, put my face into it, and wept. I told God, "I thought you were a God of love. But here I find you're a God who condemns people before they've even had a chance. Everybody's a robot."

As I battled with myself and the Lord on that lonely beach, it seemed that my heart filled with inky disillusionment. Everything I'd believed about a God of love, power, kindness, and compassion was evaporating.

Nonetheless, God was compassionate. The Spirit seemed to say to me, "Why don't you study this through on your own? Put aside your own thoughts and let Me speak to your heart."

It was almost chilling. But I agreed. The result was not only a deeper understanding of God's sovereignty, but a greater commitment to His grace and love than ever before—and without denying the truths of Scripture.

There are always those times when we discover that the God we imagined is not the God of Scripture. For instance . . .

• We encounter a biblical doctrine that bashes our inherited theology to pieces (like believer's baptism versus infant baptism). We're so distraught, we feel like tearing up our Bibles. What is worse is that as we begin studying the subject, the murk in our minds only deepens.

• We claim a promise and nothing happens. Has God reneged on His Word?

• We practice spiritual disciplines and our problems only get worse. "What happened?" we cry.

• We pray about a problem, it goes on for months, and God seems unwilling to answer. We begin to ask why, if He could part the Red Sea, He can't solve our difficulty.

Take, for example, Moses' complaint to God in Numbers 11:11-15. Read through and notice the elements inherent in such questions.

1. *We accuse God of being unfair with us.*

We say He's been "hard" and hasn't shown "favor."

Is this true? Not at all. God has taken responsibility for His people. In fact, it's possible that if, when we wanted a change of circumstances, instead of complaining to God we made a humble request, certainly He could fill it. But if our attitude is always combative, never kind, meek, or gentle, we allow sin to hinder our communication with the heavenly Father. (See

I Thessalonians 5:18 and John 9:31.)

Instead of gentle, direct requests, the disillusioned mind resorts to accusations. It assumes the worst about someone—even God—and therefore approaches with anger and a swinging bat.

2. *We exaggerate the problem completely.*

Now we may attack God. In effect, we lose sight of the real problem. When we are angry and frustrated, we don't think clearly. We tend to blow the problem into a tyrannosaurus rex when, in reality, it may not be much more than a snowshoe rabbit. We blame everyone, especially God. No one can fix it. It's hopeless. We might as well go die.

3. *We feel God has reneged on His agreement.*

We begin to doubt everything now. "You didn't give it to me—even though it's in your Word." This is resentment cranked to the breaking point. We may have taken the verse out of context or claimed a promise made to someone else, but that doesn't matter. We're hot as an acetylene torch, lit and blazing.

4. *We feel totally alone.*

If there's an absolute truth about disillusionment, it's the feeling that no one understands. They just don't see things the way you can, which you're convinced is the truth. They're all deluded. You're totally alone.

But are you? No. God has promised, "I will never desert you, nor will I ever forsake you" (Hebrews 13:5). Yes, we may *feel* alone. But feelings aren't necessarily reality or truth. No matter how we feel, we are *never* alone. God is there, ready to listen and meet a need—if only we would ask! "For we do not have a high priest who cannot sympathize with our weaknesses, but one who has been tempted in all things as we are, yet without sin. Let us therefore draw near with confidence to the throne of grace, that we may receive mercy and may find grace to help in time of need" (Hebrews 4:15-16).

5. *We'd rather die.*

This is the ultimate end of all disillusionment—depression. "Kill me, God. I can't take any more of this." In effect, it's the ultimate in self-pity. "You won't play my way? Then kill me. I don't care."

The disillusioned person doesn't want to die so much as to have God make everything right—NOW! He's simply trying to make God feel badly that He treated him this way. It's manipulation. Nothing more. Nothing less.

Coming To Grips

How, then, do we come to grips with this problem of expectations and God not fulfilling them?

First, realize that God's thoughts and ways aren't our thoughts and ways. Remember Isaiah 55:8-9? " 'My thoughts are not your thoughts, neither are your ways My ways,' declares the Lord. 'For as the heavens are higher than the earth, so are My ways higher than your ways.' " The whole of the Christian life is to bring our minds and hearts in line with God's mind and heart. The world, the flesh, and the devil are all working overtime to eliminate the truth from our hearts (I John 2:15-17). In addition, they're doing everything they can to pour in falsehood. So be prepared to have plenty of traditions shattered and convictions realigned. The moment you're born again, you aren't given the whole package. It takes a lifetime to get yourself safely entrenched in the "narrow" way.

Second, study the Scriptures through. I like what Paul said to Timothy in II Timothy 2:15. "Be diligent to present yourself approved to God as a workman who does not need to be ashamed, handling accurately the word of truth." Notice his emphasis: diligence; seeking God's approval (by pleasing Him above all); avoiding shame (believing or teaching falsehood); and "handling accurately" the Word. That last phrase is interesting. It's the idea of a diamond cutter who wants to be absolutely accurate in cutting a diamond. One mistake and he could lop off a whole facet. He has to be precise, cautious, careful, and exact.

That's the way to treat God's Word. We can't come to it glibly or flippantly, thinking it will divulge its depths in a "quick read." No, God's Word demands study, meditation, commitment, time, heart, and soul. The only way to prevent disillusionment is by treating God's Word with utmost reverence.

Third, understand God's purpose for disillusionment. Yes, God does want to disillusion you. That is, He wants to rid you of Satan's illusions about the world, life, death, people, salvation, and most of all, Himself. He may allow you to become disillusioned so that you're driven to find out the truth.

If disillusionment forces us to study, that study will bear fruit. We will become so grounded in God's truth that soon nothing can dissuade us of the basic tenets of our faith. Disillusionment doesn't have to break us.

Last, rejoice that God will not let us go or remain disillusioned. The Lord Jesus is committed to our growth and triumph as Christians. Philippians 1:6 assures us, "I am confident of this very thing, that He who began a good work in you will perfect it until the day of Christ Jesus." No matter how great your disillusionment, the Lord is greater (I John 3:20, 4:4). He can not only turn your darkness inside out, but He will stand you rightside up.

How will He do it? Through His Word—and sometimes through His people.

During the 1980 Olympics, Eric Heiden won the heart of America by winning five gold medals in speed skating. It was easy to cheer for and encourage this hearty symbol of American achievement.

What isn't commonly known is that in the 10,000 meter race, Heiden had already set a world record early in the heats, but there were many skaters still to follow. The very last heat involved a 17-year-old Korean lad, and he would be skating *alone*. Already the crowd was filing out to see other events. But a group of several hundred Americans decided to stay.

When the Korean competitor took off at the gun, the crowd cheered its heart out. The racer gave everything. For some time he seemed to be skating even faster than Heiden had. But the crowd cheered even more. Eventually, his pace fell off and he did not win. But to the very end, that crowd lent its voice to his sweat-engined rhythm, cheering even for a competitor because he was giving his all.

I tend to think of the church like that. When others are disillusioned, we need to come alongside, to cheer and encourage and revitalize the dormant juices. Like Jude says, "Have mercy on some, who are doubting; save others, snatching them out of the fire; and on some have mercy with fear, hating even the garment polluted by the flesh" (Jude 22-23).

Have you ever seen that V-formation of geese flying south? The reason for the V is because it cuts down on wind resistance for those who follow the leader. Throughout the flight, one goose leads for awhile, then moves back in the formation to rest while others take over.

But have you also noticed the honking? Why? It's goose-encouragement. They're telling one another to keep up, keep flying, hang in there, don't give up, don't get discouraged. We're going south; it's a real place, soon we'll be there.

That's what God's church needs for those who suffer from disillusionment: honkers who will remind them of the truth. For it's truth that rids us of the false expectations that lead us into disillusionment.

PART III: CURES

A look at the whole issue of the God who plans our
lives and the plan of God. How do you and I fit in?

12/WHO'S IN CHARGE HERE?

If there is a single key to the problem of suffering broken dreams, shattered plans, and demolished hopes, it's bound up in understanding God's sovereignty.

God's sovereignty is, in some ways, the most comforting doctrine of the Bible. It offers us hope, joy, security, and confidence for every situation of life. It's a truth precious beyond measure, and one I often turn to in trouble.

Just the same, God's sovereignty is also one of the most misunderstood, maligned, and mitigated truths you'll find in Scripture. Theologians have both hallowed it and halved it. They've explored it and deplored it. It remains a doctrine that often provokes fear, anger, hatred, and malice on the part of both believers and non-believers.

Why?

We could list a hundred reasons. But I think one is sufficient: Satan.

The devil rails against God's sovereignty more than any other doctrine, for it is His sovereignty that holds the devil in check, thwarts his evil schemes, and destroys his wicked plans. Satan will do anything to destroy that truth, even if it means simply deceiving men and women about it.

But what is God's sovereignty? What does it mean?

The Elements of Sovereignty

Sovereignty means God is Lord, Master, Ruler, King. Everyone answers to Him. He answers to no one. Everyone bows before Him. He bows before no one. Everyone depends on him. He depends on no one. He has no needs, no limitations, no fears, no hopes. He has everything under His control. Nothing catches Him by surprise. He never sleeps. No one can push Him off the throne. There is one King, and He will remain King eternally.

Though there are a multitude of Scriptures about God's sovereignty, consider just a few.

"I am the Lord, that is My name; I will not give My glory to another, nor My praise to graven images" (Isaiah 42:8).

"I am the first and I am the last, and there is no God besides Me" (Isaiah 44:6).

"I am the Lord, and there is no other, besides Me there is no God. I will gird you, though you have not known Me; that men may know from the rising to the setting of the sun that there is no one besides Me. I am the Lord and there is no other, the One forming light and creating darkness, causing well-being and creating calamity; I am the Lord who does all these" (Isaiah 45:5-7).

"The counsel of the Lord stands forever, the plans of His heart from generation to generation" (Psalm 33:11).

"Oh, the depth of the riches both of the wisdom and knowledge of God! How unsearchable are His judgments and unfathomable His ways! For who has known the mind of the Lord, or who became His counselor? Or who has first given to Him that it might be paid back to Him again? For from Him and through Him and to Him are all things" (Romans 11:33-36).

We could easily multiply these verses. Undoubtedly, every

page of the Bible contains some reference to God's sovereignty.

What It Means

But what does it mean that He is sovereign? Is it just a fancy term for saying He's king of the universe?

If you take a look at the world, it appears to be anything *but* ruled by God. Rumors of wars, wars, murders, thefts, rapes, idolatries, sorceries; you name it, they abound. In what sense is God sovereign over them? Or over any of us? We all sin. We all defy Him. People even challenge Him, saying, "If you're there, let lightning strike me dead." No lightning strikes. People sin willfully, then boast that He did nothing to stop them. The existence of sin, evil, and corruption are, in fact, one of the strongest arguments non-believers hurl at believers. "If God is there, why is there so much evil in the world? Why doesn't He do anything?"

Rabbi Harold Kushner wrote a popular book, called *Why Bad Things Happen to Good People*, on this issue. His conclusion was that God is good and loving, but evil is also powerful, and God has not yet overcome it. He's trying, but He just doesn't have that much power.

That's typical of flawed human reasoning. And frankly, it makes God just another invalid in the house. It rejects the God of all-power revealed in the Bible. Trying to reduce God to the level of man is not the answer.

Let's look at several elements of what it means biblically that God is sovereign.

In Charge

First, it means *He's in charge.* He's in control. The Scriptures earlier make that plain. "The Lord nullifies the counsel of the nations" (Psalm 33:10). "The counsel of the Lord stands forever" (33:11). Those verses mean that God stops human plans and asserts His own plan. His will *will* come to pass. What He has decreed *will* happen.

This doesn't mean that He manipulates events, people, and situations to His own ends. He doesn't cause evil or sin under any circumstances. Nor does He create situations to cause people to sin. He can't even look on sin (Habakkuk 1:13), and He never tempts anyone to sin (James 1:13). He has complete authority over evil beings, and they cannot do anything which He, in His wisdom, doesn't choose to allow. And for reasons known only to Himself, He has chosen to *allow* evil to run its course in this world during this time.

How is He in charge over evil? In many ways. He limits evil. He stops it. He judges it. He knows all about it before it happens, and He has included it in His overall plan— complete with judgment already decided. But He never manipulates it, or influences people to act evilly.

Because God is all-wise, He knows the end from the beginning. He knows the results of evil; sometimes He allows it as testing, punishment, judgment, or to stir His people to action for Him. Other times only He knows "why." But in faith we can trust that God is still in control. He knew what action would take place before it happened. He could have stopped it, but He didn't. He allowed it to happen (just as God allowed Titus to destroy Jerusalem in 70 A.D.) for reasons known only to Himself. He could have stopped it before anything happened. But He didn't. He chose not to.

Does that make God a perpetrator of evil? No. We're not dealing with sinless, innocent people, nor are we dealing with a sinless world. Rather, we're in a situation where sin has affected everyone and where everyone has chosen to sin.

That makes the situation very different. God has declared that the earth and everyone in it have been tainted by evil. Thus, when we speak of God's sovereignty over the world, we're speaking of an utterly unique situation. God is sovereign over a planet where all of the beings under His authority are in active rebellion against Him.

Think of it. Imagine being lifeguard at a pool where everyone inside declares from the start that they're not going to listen to you, believe you, like you, or obey you. Then imagine telling that group that regardless of their threats and taunts, you're still in charge, and you have no intention of abdicating your position.

That's God's sovereignty. He has told us, "You may refuse to listen to Me or obey Me, but that changes nothing. I'm still in control."

Just because the world looks anarchic and people all over the world defy God, it changes nothing. Only if God chooses to abdicate His throne can the world start saying He's not sovereign. His plan, His counsels, His predetermined blueprint are what is happening in the world. Even if we can't see Him, or feel Him, or even sense His work and control in our lives, He's still there. He's still in charge.

Second, *sovereignty means everything happens according to God's predetermined plan.* Someone may say, "That sounds like predestination to me." Yes. God made a plan before anything ever happened. Several verses of Scripture attest to this. Isaiah 46:9-11 declares, "Remember the former things long past, for I am God, and there is no other; I am God, and there is no one like Me, declaring the end from the beginning and from ancient times things which have not been done, saying, 'My purpose will be established, and I will accomplish all My good pleasure.' " Psalm 90:2, Proverbs 8:23-31, Isaiah 43:7,10-11, Micah 5:2, II Timothy 1:9, and Titus 1:2 are just a few others. That plan included everything that would ever happen in the universe. Everything. God knew it in infinite detail before He ever created an atom. He knew precisely what would take place, where, and when to the microsecond.

God is the manager of the universe, and every thing and being in it—from the amoeba to the orangutan, from the paramecium to the platypus. Remember what Jesus said? He knows when the sparrow falls and the number of hairs on our heads. Nothing escapes His notice.

If you regard these things as incredible, perhaps the problem is that your image of God is too small. That's why He will not give His glory to another. Why should He? His greatness so towers over us that we're mere specks in comparison.

But someone might say, "If His plan includes evil, then He must be evil."

Not at all. Just because He has allowed evil to be part of the blueprint doesn't mean He's the cause of that evil. Does a baseball coach want his batters to strike out? Does a football coach want his quarterback to get sacked? Of course not. But the coach knows those things will happen and has a plan to deal with them when they do. God, however, knows precisely where and when our strikes and fumbles will occur. That, however, does not make Him the cause of those strikes and errors, nor does it make Him blameable.

Third, *sovereignty means no one can circumvent God's plan*. His plan stands. That's why the Psalm says, "The counsel of the Lord stands forever, the plans of His heart from generation to generation" (33:11). It includes every variation, every action, every thought, every word. No one can stop Him or it. It's as relentless as sunrise, as sure as starlight. What He planned in eternity happens in time exactly as recorded.

The fact is, though, that no one knows God's plan in detail. We can know only those things He's revealed in the Bible. Everything else is part of His secret counsel (Deuteronomy 29:29). So, in a sense, we can't know what God's plan is until it's history. It's useless to speak in terms of evading God's plans, or circumventing them, or overturning them, or messing them up.

There's an old expression about God's Word: "The Bible is an anvil that has worn out many hammers." That's an example of God's sovereignty. Through the ages, tyrants, kings, dictators, and persecutors have tried to eradicate the Bible not only from existence, but also from the minds and hearts of people. It hasn't happened. It never will. Why? Because the "grass withers, the flower fades, but the Word of God stands forever" (Isaiah 40:8).

One day as I was eating an apple, I suddenly stopped and said, "God knew that I would eat this apple, at this time, before the foundation of the world."

A friend answered, "Doesn't that make you feel locked in?"

I had to think about that. Then I realized that no, I don't feel locked in. Rather, it makes me rejoice. It reminds me that I have a Lord so concerned about all my needs that He knows precisely how and when they'll be met. In fact, as Christians we have a Lord who—far from locking us in—sets us free to true life because we need have no fear that we'll ever face anything we can't handle—in the power of the Holy Spirit. That's tremendously freeing. That gives hope. That's why Paul could say, "No temptation has overtaken you but such as is common to man; and God is faithful, who will not allow you to be tempted beyond what you are able; but with the temptation will provide the way of escape also, that you may be able to endure it" (I Corinthians 10:13). How could Paul say that unless God is sovereign?

Take Ephesians 2:10: "For we are His workmanship, created in Christ Jesus for good works, which God prepared beforehand, that we should walk in them." God has planned our lives to be full of opportunities to do good. Those opportunities are specific, tailored to our interests and desires, and hand-selected according to our abilities. How could Paul say that unless God is truly in charge of history?

Still, someone might say, "What about human freedom? What about choices? Are we robots?"

That's the fourth point about God's sovereignty. *Sovereignty includes human freedom and the power to make real choices.*

There is a sense in which every one of our wills is bound to our sinful nature. We act in accordance with that nature and cannot, even by force, choose right, good, the truth, or Christ without the Lord's intervention.

But there's another sense in which we're free to make real choices without coercion. God does not force us to choose Christ, nor does He manipulate us into making a decision we don't want to make. Because He is God, He can work within us through the power of the Holy Spirit without violating our humanity or our will.

Take the example of the crucifixion of Christ. Luke records in the book of Acts that all this occurred under God's sovereignty. Herod, Pilate, the Gentiles, and Jews did "whatever Thy hand and Thy purpose predestined to occur" (Acts 4:28). That's the sovereignty side of it. But they made those choices without coercion from above.

That's why it's critical for us to understand and believe that God's plan includes everything—even our choices of things like spouse, job, career, home, and so on. He has not only planned that we have such choices, but He's planned what choices we'll make—without violating any of our personal freedom or right to choose.

"Impossible," some say.

It appears that way. But that actually demonstrates the greatness of God's sovereignty and our faith. He, as our Lord and Master, is so powerful and great that He is above and beyond our simple choices. He never forces us to do anything. He never manipulates us. He never violates our own heart and soul decisions. And yet, He has incorporated it in a magnificent, all-inclusive plan that will be to His and our ultimate glory and highest benefit. He laid out that plan before we ever existed.

"But how can it be?" some say.

I don't know. That's part of the mystery and greatness of God. It's part of what makes Him worthy of our love and worship. If we could explain God, He would no longer be God.

Think of it. Suppose we all had complete freedom of choice to do as we pleased, but there was no sovereign God. What would happen? Chaos. Anarchy. And all of us, because of our sin, would end up destroying one another.

But sovereignty prevents that. God guides it all so that anarchy and chaos never gain control. And He does it without turning us into robots.

God's sovereignty includes free choice every step of the way. It's not tyrannical or dictatorial. Everyone who comes to love Him, in the end, will say, "You have done all things perfectly, Lord." Only through freedom can there be things like love, worship, kindness, patience, caring. But only through sovereignty can there be security, hope, safety, and joy. He's created a situation in which both are in force, and both provide the depths and heights of life. That's His glory. That's His greatness.

Fifth, and last, *sovereignty includes human responsibility.* Our tendency is to think, "If God is sovereign and in total control, then everything I do is controlled and caused by Him. Therefore, I'm not really responsible for anything I do."

But sovereignty does incorporate human responsibility into the plan. God maintains control without ever causing us to make wrong choices or leading us into evil. When we sin, we're responsible for it. Likewise, when we do good, He will reward us, because we made the right choice. He incorporated all these choices into His plan, but He didn't override our responsibility to obey on our own.

Paul dealt with this issue in Romans 9. He spoke of Pharaoh and how God had raised Pharaoh up in order to "demonstrate My power in you, and that My name might be proclaimed throughout the whole earth" (Romans 9:17).

Pharaoh rejected Moses' plea that Israel be set free. Why? In several places it says he "hardened" his heart (Exodus 8:15, 8:32, 9:34). That is, he chose to be merciless; he refused to let their plight affect him, and he chose to reject their request. In other places, it says Pharaoh's heart "was hardened," without saying who did what (7:13, 8:19, 9:7, 9:35).

But in at least fourteen instances, either God Himself says, "I will harden his heart," or the text says, "God hardened his heart." (See such passages as Exodus 4:21, 9:12, 10:1, 10:20, 10:27; 11:10.) Does this mean Pharaoh was not, therefore, guilty for his sin in rejecting Israel's request?

No, not at all. That would make Pharaoh an automaton in God's hands. The Bible is clear that God made us in His image. He is not a robot; neither are we.

To explain this situation, someone has said, "The same sun that melts wax hardens clay." Sunlight is good, benign, even neutral. If you place a bit of wax out on the pavement on a 90 degree day, that wax will melt. If you put a piece of clay in the same place, it will harden. Likewise, God's goodness shone on two hearts—Moses' and Pharaoh's. Moses' heart melted. He repented, turned to God, and accepted Him. Pharaoh, on the other hand, hardened like that clay.

God knows precisely what will happen if He pours out His love and goodness on some people: they'll become harder, angrier, more implacable than ever. On others, they'll warm up to Him and change under His power.

All of us have seen this in human relations. Haven't you ever been angry with someone, and they, in trying to make things right, treat you with extra kindness? What happens? In many cases, you relent, smile, and you're good friends again. But what if you're so angry deep down inside that you refuse to give in? In effect, you "harden" your heart. How might you respond to your friend's efforts at reconciliation and goodness? You might say, "He's just doing it because he feels guilty. Well, I'm mad. I'm not giving in." Or you might rationalize it, "He's faking it just to get his way. He doesn't really care about me."

Remember the two thieves crucified with Jesus on Calvary? One repented. The other hurled insults. Both saw everything Jesus did on that cross. Both had the same information. But only one repented. Why? The melting/hardening process. Some people melt in the face of God's love; others harden.

God overwhelmed Pharaoh with warnings, pleas, requests, prophecies. But Pharaoh became more furious, more stubborn, more pugnacious. He didn't care who God was. He wasn't going to give in to God.

So what was God's overriding purpose in all this hardening? Exodus 14:18. "Then the Egyptians will know that I am the Lord, when I am honored through Pharaoh, through his chariots and the horseman." God's purpose was to make Himself known. The first thing God has to do in bringing people to Himself is to make them aware of their need, of their sin and guilt, of their lostness. That's what God was doing in hardening Pharaoh, trying to turn him from his sin. But Pharaoh chose to ignore the many signs of God's power.

The point is that God didn't make Pharaoh sin. He simply took what was already there—a stubborn, sinful, hateful heart—and, by exposing it to His majesty, it became harder.

Thus, God's sovereignty includes man's responsibility. God may have to fire every bullet He possesses to get us to take an action. He might drop a spiritual A-bomb. Or, He might warm us with sunlight, lap gentle waves at our feet, and roast us golden on a beautiful beach. But His purpose is change, transformation, getting us to do what's right, not forcing us to do what's wrong (Romans 8:28-31). And if, in the end, we choose to fight God to the death, we're responsible for that, too. Sovereignty means God knew what He was doing from beginning to end, and the final result was part of His eternal plan. He was never stymied in any part of the process.

Why Believe It?

Why should you or I believe these truths?

If you read a daily newspaper, watch the evening news, or simply keep abreast of events in our world, there are many human reasons to question the idea of God's sovereignty. How can God be good, loving, all-powerful, and holy—and let the kinds of things happen in our world that happen nearly every day? We think He should stop evil entirely, judge it now, or at least take some action. Something!

What we fail to consider is that if God decided to terminate evil today, which of us would be left tomorrow? When He judges evil, it will be once and for all!

That doesn't mean that God has done nothing about evil, though. God could judge evil today, but He has decided to postpone that final judgment until a later date (II Peter 2—3). He could have stopped Lucifer the moment he turned over his first nasty thought. He could judge individuals the second they commit sin—or even the moment before. But He has chosen to allow evil to run its course. He has chosen, in His sovereignty, to deal with evil in an all-encompassing, final way that will insure that no one, ever again forever, will rebel against Him and bring the carnage Satan has wreaked on the world. First, He dealt with it at the cross of Christ. He placed on Jesus the sins of mankind so that any person who believes in Him can be forgiven, redeemed, transformed, and made fit for heaven. Those who reject Christ will undergo the second aspect of His verdict on evil—the Last Judgment (Revelation 20—22). But until then, evil and sin will continue to run rampant in our world. It's a situation that causes many to reject or question the idea of a sovereign God.

I know well how they feel.

One day I walked around our local mall praying and meditating, feeling broken and despondent because of problems I was facing. I found myself saying, "Please, Lord, just give me a word of reassurance."

The Lord did.

As I walked, I suddenly remembered a verse in Romans 8: "The Spirit Himself bears witness with our spirit that we are children of God" (verse 16). I turned that statement over and over in my mind, and suddenly I realized that the Spirit Himself was reminding me, "You are My child. I love you. I brought you here. And I will lead you from this place. My plan is glory."

How can anyone explain it? It's something mysterious but precious. God's sovereign presence is real, and it's personal.

You ask, "Why do you believe in God's sovereignty?" I could give many reasons: because the Bible teaches it; because I've seen it and experienced it; because I've heard and read of others testifying to it.

But I have to come back to this one. The Christian believes in God's sovereignty primarily because the Spirit Himself has persuaded him—through the Word, through others— personally. That's the glory of the life of faith. It's personal. It's down to earth. It's where we are.

Our Response To This

How, then, should we respond to these truths as they relate to our own lives and plans?

Let me offer five responses to God's sovereignty every

Christian should make.

1. Awe. If all this is true about God, and it is, then God is majestic, great beyond words, beyond explanations, beyond knowledge. What can we do in His presence? Offer words of highest praise? Of course. Tell others about Him? Certainly. But awe, that's something else. Awe is not *wow*. Awe is not starry-eyed wonder. Awe is a sense of profound and reverent fear. It's a sense of being in the presence of someone so great you dare not even whisper unless He allows you. It's a sense of being near someone so majestic that all you want to do is bow before Him and praise Him with all your heart.

2. Trust. Since God is truly sovereign, then we have every reason to trust Him. We owe Him our confidence. He is absolutely trustworthy. He has done everything to benefit us.

3. Obedience. Sovereignty means we owe Him our absolute obedience. No arguments. No tricks. No running off and hiding. His will is our command.

4. Hope. More than this, we have hope. God desires that we find in Him the highest hope possible. There's no reason to despair or give up. The Lord of the universe is on our side, if we're on His. God *can* work, *will* work, and *is* working even now on your behalf and on my behalf.

5. Action. But above all, sovereignty means action. We might tend to think that because God is sovereign we should all become passive and just "let it happen." Some people say that, because it's all ordained, why pray? But that's not it at all. Because God is sovereign it means He can work, He can act, He can change people from the inside out; He can change the course of events, history, a destiny. The fact that we pray implies God is sovereign. For if He isn't, why pray? If He isn't sovereign, He can't do anything anyway.

But sovereignty calls for prayer. Remember Jesus' words?

"Ask, and it shall be given to you; seek, and you shall find; knock, and it shall be opened to you." That's action. That's trust. That's knowing God can do something.

In fact, some of the most influential men and women of God through the ages have been those who believed acutely in God's sovereignty.

Charles Spurgeon, famed English preacher of the 19th century, was a fervent preacher of God's sovereignty. He pled with men to repent. He exhorted them repeatedly. He marshalled every illustration, every facet of articulation, every piece of wisdom and power to turn hearts to God. Why? Because he believed God could change people, bring them to their knees, turn them around. That's sovereignty.

Adoniram Judson went to Burma to lead "the heathen" to Christ. He labored for years learning the language, compiling dictionaries, translating the Bible. Converts came slowly, the first only after years in the work. But Judson believed God would act, that He would break the bonds of sin. God's sovereignty drove him to greater action.

Eric Liddell loved His sovereign Lord and chose not to run his event—the 100 meters—in the 1924 Olympics because the qualifying heats were run on a Sunday. He had trained for that event. He held records in it. He was slated to win. But he obeyed God, not man. Was it all over for him? No, the sovereign God had something better planned. Eric ran the 200 meters and won a silver. Then he ran the 400 and won the gold. Because of his flailing, all out unique style of running, he was the hit of the games. God, in His sovereignty, exalted His man and His witness for Christ.

Corrie ten Boom went to Ravensbruck concentration camp in 1944. She might have rejected her faith, complaining that a sovereign God wouldn't do this to her or her family. But she didn't. She continued to believe even though civilization was exploding before her eyes. Her whole family died in those camps. But Corrie survived. She came out to tell the world her story, boiled down to one line: "There is no pit so deep that God is not deeper still."

But perhaps the Apostle Paul was the greatest sovereignty preacher of all. His Lord was a Lord of action, a Lord with power, a Lord of change. So he put his biblical sword in his hand and marched. Acts records the drumbeat. In Damascus, the Jews plotted to kill him. That didn't stop Paul. He escaped in a basket and went to Jerusalem. The Jerusalem Christians feared him. But Paul befriended Barnabas and finally found acceptance in the brotherhood. Paul went to Antioch and established the church there. But that wasn't enough. He wanted to take the message to the whole world. He and Barnabas set out on the first missionary journey. They were greeted with rejection, persecution, hatred. But that didn't stop them. Their God was sovereign. They established churches throughout Galatia. They went to Iconium where the Jews tried to stone them. That couldn't stop them. They fled to other cities and established more churches. First Corinthians 11:21-33 provides the cadence. They beat him with rods. They stoned him. They whipped him with a cat o' nine tails five times. But none of these things stopped him. Paul had a God who was sovereign. He would press on.

Sovereignty is a reason to rejoice, to hope, to trust, and, above all, to act. Pray. Witness. Give. Start ministries. Serve the Lord. Why? Because He will take those things, use them, and spread His kingdom. It will never be stopped. Why? Because He is Lord. He is God. He is Sovereign.

What If?

But what if you and God disagree? What if your plans fizzle, and His plan has you frazzled?

Good question. That's what this book is about—when God's plan and your plan conflict. That's why we have to move on to a second issue: what is God's plan? What does it include? How can I know God's plan—and believe that it's better than my plan?

Let's look at that in the next chapter.

13/WHAT KIND OF COVERAGE ARE WE TALKING HERE?

The first time I walked into our field service manager's office, I was astounded to see a chart filling the whole left wall of the room. I asked him what it was.

"It's a flow chart," he said. "It pinpoints the whole flow of operations for the installation of a corrugator."

A corrugator is a three hundred-thirty foot series of machines that turn rolls of brown paper into sandwiched sheets of corrugated board used to make boxes. Our company makes those machines and sells them to boxmakers. Putting one of those monsters in, though, requires the utmost in planning and management skill.

Thus, the field service flow chart.

I took a closer look at its intricate design. Sure enough, there were the individual operations I had been long familiar with, everything from building the containers to hold the machines so they could be shipped, to pushing the button that whirred a completed machine into producing boxboard at one thousand feet per minute. It was astonishing. Arrows all over the place, from one step to the next. Time lapses. A series of operations, lined up, then a gap—I suppose a giant yawn in the 18 hour days some men put in.

It staggered me to see what planning went into getting a corrugator up and running.

How much more staggering to realize what it took for God to know everything that would occur in His universe from the first jagged jolt of light in the beginning to the final clop of

the horses' hooves at the end.
What is this plan that God has fashioned?

What It Includes

When we speak of God's plan, it's different from His "will." God's will refers to His decreed laws and principles about how to conduct ourselves righteously in His universe. We call this His "revealed will" or His "moral will." The Bible contains all of it. If we want to know what His will is on an issue, we turn to Scripture. If we find there's nothing specific about our problem, we act on the basis of the principles He's revealed.

On the other hand, there's God's plan, that marvelous blueprint on which He has laid out all the things that come to pass in history. Every comet that has scorched its way across the heavens. Every meteorite that has made a white slide through earth's atmosphere. Every robin warble. Every mosquito bite. Every baby's "Maaa-maaa!" Every bullet, every light switch, every printed word on the page. It's all there on the blueprint in God's mind. He sketched in every detail before He ever spoke the words, "Let there be light."

This plan is His secret. No one knows it but Him. Only those things He's already revealed in the Scriptures are certain. Everything else is hidden. What He has not revealed, we cannot know. If He has decreed that the stock market will crash on September 5, 1996, it will crash. But we can't know it until it happens. On the other hand, He has told us the Antichrist will arise and control the world for seven years. That's something we don't have to speculate about. He has told us about a few events that will happen in the future not only to warn us, but to arouse faith. When we see come to pass what He told us in advance would happen, we believe.

Let me suggest several things God's plan includes . . .

1. Everything about you and everyone else—physically, mentally, emotionally.

God personally formed and fashioned you and me. He gave us everything we have—every talent, gift, ability, every part of our physical makeup: the color of our eyes, the strength of our intellect, even our personality. We might think we're the product of genetics or chance or environment. But not so. "Thou didst form my inward parts; Thou didst weave me in my mother's womb" (Psalm 139:13). If you're ever tempted to put yourself down, stop. God made you the way you are. He chose every thing about you—where you were born, your parents, how you would grow, what interests you would develop. He gave you all the tools and talents you have.

"But I have so many faults."

His plan included them.

"But I don't like what I see."

That's your fallenness. When God said, "It is good," He meant you and me, too.

"But there are so many things I wish I could change about myself."

Perhaps. We should always seek to become more Christlike. But those unchangeable features of ourselves, God gave us for a reason. In His wisdom, He made us the way we are. And in His wisdom, He will perfect us. The thing we need to do is to stop complaining about the work of God—us—and start giving thanks that He is our Lord. We are His personal work of art. We are one of His displays in the heavenly Louvre. Ask Him how He feels about you and He says, "You are fearfully and wonderfully made." That means that each of us is one of His magnificent achievements. Man is the "crown of creation," and we are the jewels of that crown (Psalm 8:5).

His sovereignty extends to the timbre of your voice, the whorls on your fingertips, and the fact that you like to sing in the shower or climb mountains. Make no mistake about it,

God takes pride in His work; you are no exception.

2. *Every thought, word, and deed, both good and bad.*

"For His dominion is an everlasting dominion, and His kingdom endures from generation to generation. And all the inhabitants of the earth are accounted as nothing, but He does according to His will in the host of heaven and among the inhabitants of the earth; and no one can ward off His hand or say to Him, 'What hast Thou done?' " (Daniel 4:34-35).

Some might be skeptical about the idea that His plan includes every deed, word, and *thought.* But consider several verses. First, Proverbs 21:1: "The king's heart is like channels of water in the hand of the Lord; He turns it wherever He wishes." Clearly, God has control over a heart from which comes both good and evil (Proverbs 23:7; Philippians 4:8).

We saw this in the example of Pharaoh when Moses sought to free Israel from Egypt. God warned Moses that Pharaoh would not respond to his request. Then, God worked through Pharaoh so that all Egypt might see His power and glory through the miracles. It was actually an act of grace. He sought to bring them to faith.

In Ezra 6:22 the prophet writes: "They observed the Feast of Unleavened Bread seven days with joy, for the Lord had caused them to rejoice, and had turned the heart of the king of Assyria toward them to encourage them in the work of the house of God." God "turned the heart of the king."

I recall many times in my Christian life when I was prompted to do something because something inside my head kept suggesting I do it. Recently, I was driving home in the snow, and suddenly, the car felt different. The rear tire was making a strange noise I'd never heard before. I thought it must be the road or the snow because I wasn't getting a bumpy ride like a flat would produce. But something kept saying inside my head, "You'd better stop and check it." I finally pulled over. Sure enough, I had a flat.

Where did that prompting come from? God—whether through the commonsense He gave me or His Spirit.

Our fallen nature dominates every word, thought, and deed until we become Christians. Even when we're born again, we don't shed that evil influence totally. Rather, we enter the warring arena of God and Satan, and both vie for our attention and obedience. That's a strong reason why we need the armor of God detailed in Ephesians 6:10-17. It's like what Paul said in Galatians 5:17, "For the flesh sets its desire against the Spirit, and the Spirit against the flesh; for these are in opposition to one another, so that you may not do the things that you please."

What did Paul mean? Once you become a Christian, the Holy Spirit comes to reside within you and directly influences every thought. At the same time, Satan works externally, trying to get you to rebel. What happens? Say you're tempted to hedge on your tax returns. On the one hand, Satan's at your left hand suggesting you cheat here, hedge there, put in a higher figure on this line, and so on. At the same time, the Spirit's speaking and reminding you of God's Word, seeking to turn you from that evil direction. The result is that "you may not do the things that you please." You feel stymied, unable to go in any direction. You can't do what you'd like to do—save a little money by cheating. But you feel the pain of paying all that extra money to do what's right.

So what is Paul's answer? You'll find it in Galatians 5:16. "Walk by the Spirit, and you will not carry out the desire of the flesh." Give the Spirit free rein. Let Him lead. Obey His directives, and the frustration is gone. Through submission, we're set free from the pain of feeling pulled in different directions. However, that struggle will go on throughout your life. In fact, it's one thing that assures us that we're Christians, for if we weren't, we'd face little struggle against sin at all.

What does this have to do with God and His plan for your life?

The Lord's plan includes both the Spirit's leading and the devil's temptations. God works directly through His Spirit. He has allowed Satan to be the prince of the power of the air. Satan tempts and tries to deceive us. But God simply works around his evil actions.

How can this be? How, then, can God include so much in His plan, even our thoughts?

It's beyond any of us. It's unimaginable. It requires an infinite mind capable of handling infinite data. It calls for an omnipotent mind able to work inside people. It mandates a loving mind because so much care is required in working within each individual. It demands a holy mind, unswerving in its rejection and hatred of evil. And it dictates a restraining mind, one that allows us to keep our identity, individuality, and freedom even as He works in us.

That's the key. God has done all this without destroying our selfhood in the least. That is the greatness of God—who does all things perfectly.

3. A beginning, a middle, and an end.

Any novelist knows his story must contain three elements: a beginning, a middle, and an end. God's plan started before the creation of the heavens and the earth. It moved on through human history, and it's leading everything to a dramatic conclusion.

Think about the drama of it. God creates angelic beings possessing incredible beauty and power. One-third of those beings rebel against Him, eventually causing mankind to rebel. He planned for that, but now He has two rebellions on His hands. He continues with His plan and begins the process of redeeming humanity from certain death. He takes the world along the paths of history. He chooses a man to become the head of a nation who will proclaim Him to all others (that's Abraham). He raises up leaders and prophets to further the story. He assures them a Redeemer is coming.

Then that Redeemer comes: Jesus. He displays wondrous powers. He speaks words that burn in men's hearts.

Then, suddenly, He's killed.

But it's still part of a plan. Jesus rises from the dead. His disciples start a worldwide movement. It goes on for centuries.

Then, God takes all the believers out of the world. The restraining power of the Holy Spirit is gone. No one around to worship. "What now?" ask the angels. "Looks like everything's over."

No, it's just another chapter. An incredible time of tribulation highlights the greatest revival in history alongside the pinnacle of rebellion.

Then Jesus comes back, stops the rebellion, destroys all the rebels, and starts a new kingdom with those who love Him. He reigns on earth for a thousand years.

But then the thousand years are up, and there's *another* rebellion. "What on earth is this?" ask the angels.

Just another means to show that even when Satan is held back, God reigns, and people see Him face to face, they still have stony hearts.

But then God stops that rebellion, judges all the rebels once and for all, and begins a new heaven and earth. They reign together forever and ever.

What a story! Is that enough drama for you? Enough action? It's certainly better than some of the sagas that make the bestseller lists. Yet, that's the plotline of God's plan. It has a beginning, a middle, and an end. And you and I are right in the center of it!

4. An overarching purpose.

"The counsel of the Lord stands forever, the plans of His heart from generation to generation" (Psalm 33:11).

God does everything for a reason. He didn't just whip up a universe one day and say, "Hey, this'll be fun." He wasn't bored or tinkering around in His shed. Everything has purpose. God does not act on whim. He knows where He's taking us, and why. We'll look at that in chapter 14.

5. God's plan contains principles and laws that may be obeyed or disobeyed.

God has given us a multitude of principles and laws in Scripture that we can take or leave, obey or disobey. These compose elements of His "revealed" or "moral" will. They are guidelines we can use in the context of our lives. While His eternal plan includes everything that will happen, His moral will reveals what we should do in any given situation. If we want to marry an unbeliever, He's told us His will on that issue (II Corinthians 6:14). If we are tempted to shoplift from the local store, we have other commands to guide us (Matthew 19:18, Ephesians 4:28).

His moral will makes us responsible. His eternal plan knows precisely what we will do.

6. It includes real choices.

We looked at this in the previous chapter. But remember this, His plan includes choices that are real to us, in our frame of reference. When we face a decision, we may consider a number of options, make charts, pray, seek guidance, study Scripture, hope for a sign from heaven, or tear at our bald spot in frustration. God's eternal plan includes all the dramatics, setbacks, tricks, cul-de-sacs, and problems we encounter. When we make our choice, it's real. We have complete freedom—carrying responsibility for the consequences. We're only constrained insofar as our judgment, knowledge, and personal depravity limit us. We're bound only to our convictions. But we make that choice freely. The choice we make was the one in His eternal plan.

7. *It includes the right to influence God to change His plan.*

Remember when God threatened to destroy the people of Israel after they worshiped the golden calf in Exodus 32? He told Moses He'd make of Moses a whole new nation and start again from scratch. Moses begged God not to do that, and, wonder of wonders, the text says God "changed His mind about the harm which He said He would do to His people" (Exodus 32:14). We see the same thing in Jonah 3:9.

Moses changed God's mind?! The people of Nineveh moved the Creator of the universe?!

From our point of view, from the standpoint of prayer and God's Word, this seems a contradiction to verses such as Malachi 3:6, I Samuel 15:29, and Hebrews 7:21. But God constantly invites us to take part in bringing His plan about. Even to the point of supposedly changing His mind.

Have you ever thought of prayer as a means to influence God, to actually affect people's destinies? That's precisely what it is. Talking to God in prayer is God's ordained means of moving Him to action in human history. "Ask, and it shall be given to you," Jesus said (Matthew 7:7). "Therefore I say to you, all things for which you pray and ask, believe that you have received them, and they shall be granted you" (Mark 11:24).

That's what we're doing when we kneel by our beds, or talk to the Lord in our car, or in church, or wherever. We're seeking to influence God. To do what? To take action. To change things. To rectify a situation. To alter history. In effect, to change what we see happening around us.

Name any saint in human history who prayed, and you'll find that's precisely what he or she wanted to do. Even Jesus sought to change the Father's mind at one point, asking Him to let "this cup pass from Me." He didn't want to go to the cross. But in the end, He also said, "Yet not as I will, but as Thou wilt" (Matthew 26:39).

That's a strange paradox. We marshall our arguments, present the facts, offer reasonable reasons, and plead with Him to grant our request, but in the end we must conclude, "Yet, not what I want, but Thy will be done." Sometimes He does what we desire. Sometimes He doesn't. God is immutable—unchanging—and eternal, holy, perfect, wise, and omniscient. But the reality is that God's eternal plan even includes a sense in which He allows us to participate in its formulation and actually change it. We can influence God to take action in some situation. "The effective prayer of a righteous man can accomplish much" (James 5:16).

Think of it. We have the power to influence the God of creation. In fact, God has invited us to do that very thing. "And this is the confidence which we have before Him, that, if we ask anything according to His will, He hears us. And if we know that He hears us in whatever we ask, we know that we have all requests which we have asked from Him" (I John 5:14-15 *cf.* James 4:2-3). What more do we need do but begin asking?

8. The means as well as the end.

God has not only ordained where we're going but how we'll get there. This is why our active participation in His plan is so important. He not only ordained that Aunt Edna be unsaved at age 45, but also that you pray for her and witness to her, and she be converted at 52. He not only planned that you be in the ministry, but that you'd desire to be and would train for it. He not only blueprinted the places the nails would go in the foyer of your new church, but who would drive them and what hammer he'd use.

This is why we should never think sovereignty means we can be lazy, lax, prayerless, or derelict in our duties as Christians. God not only ordains that we be transformed, but that the ways we would be transformed would be through things like having a regular quiet time, serving in the church, listening to sermons, and helping others. God has ordained both the ends and the means to those ends.

Our Response to All of This

God—who is omniscient, perfect, wise, holy, omnipotent—is totally beyond our comprehension. That's where faith comes in. We can't understand it or Him. But we can accept what happens and who we are as coming from Him, a Person of the highest integrity and authority. What does He require of us? That we be found faithful. That we trust Him.

So what do you do now? Worship, yes. Be full of awe. Praise Him.

That's the kind of response God is looking for. That's why He gave us the Bible. Sure, He'll answer your questions. He'll try to help you to understand. But ultimately, He desires our worship, our love, our praise, our complete trust. Not that He needs those things, but He wants us to see that His plan is best and that He is worthy of our worship. Once the whole plan has played out, once we've seen it in the daylight of eternity, we'll agree, "Thou hast done all things well."

But there's an important question here. What is behind God's plan? What truths and characteristics of Himself govern how the plan came about? Let's catalog some of the personal qualities that God possesses that make Him capable of bringing off this plan.

14/WHY THE BUCK STOPS WITH GOD

Why should I trust God? Why should I believe that His plans for me and everyone else are so admirable?

Let's take a short cruise through a number of God's attributes that are critical for us to understand. They are attributes which should cause our love and reverence for the Father, Son, and Spirit to increase and abound.

God's Unique Abilities

When theologians speak of God's attributes, they often divide them into categories such as communicable (those which humans can share and understand) and incommunicable (those which humans cannot fathom). Others distinguish them as His absolute and relative attributes, or immanent and transitive. I'd like to classify them this way: His unique attributes (those characteristics only He possesses) and His transferable attributes (those which we can experience). Let's deal with these only as they relate to His plan and His sovereignty over the universe.

Omniscience

The first attribute is *omniscience*. It means "all-knowing." God's knowledge encompasses the universe and eternity.

Sovereignty implies omniscience. For God to be truly in control, He has to know everything there is to know. Psalm 139 portrays this attribute. The Lord has "searched me and known me. Thou dost know when I sit down and when I rise up; Thou dost understand my thought from afar. Thou dost scrutinize my path and my lying down, and art intimately acquainted with all my ways. Even before there is a word on my tongue, behold, O Lord, Thou dost know it all. Thou hast enclosed me behind and before, and laid Thy hand upon me. Such knowledge is too wonderful for me; it is too high, I cannot attain to it" (Psalm 139:1-6).

Look at it again. God knows everything going on inside of David—his thoughts, his ideas, his dreams, his fears. He understands him completely. He knows everything behind David's actions, why he does what he does, what experiences have shaped him and led him to act in certain ways.

Moreover, He's "intimately acquainted with all his ways." He knows the things only David knows, his innermost and most secret thoughts. Those things he may even wish God didn't know, God knows.

Omniscience means God knows all the facts as well as the emotions. Jesus said He knows the number of hairs on our heads (Matthew 10:30). His knowledge is complete, instantaneous, and effortless. He just knows.

Even we do that. If someone asks me how many children I have, I don't have to stop and count on my fingers. "Now let's see, there's Nicole, and . . . Yes, I have one."

No, I know instantly. The difference between us and God is that at a certain point we can't handle the overload. The sheer vastness of knowledge becomes too great for our minds. That's where God's omniscience becomes so astonishing to us; it's on such an enormous scale, we tend not to believe it. "How can God know the number of sand grains on Jones Beach? How can He know the stars by name? How can He know how many blades of grass are on the Buckingham Palace lawn? How can He know every thought every person has had from the beginning of time?" Frankly, I don't understand how. But He does. That's the immensity and greatness of God.

But God's omniscience isn't simply knowledge of facts. In

addition, He knows all the possibilities, all the options and alternatives. For instance, He knows every variation on the universe there is. He knows what any one of us would have been like if He'd had us born in Africa, China, West Germany, or anywhere else. He knows what would have happened had we started life in the first century, third century, or twenty-first century. He knows how it would have been for us in every race, time, situation, and parentage.

Someone might say, "But that defies statistics. You're talking about combinations and variations that are infinite."

That's precisely it. God's knowledge is infinite. We can accept it and believe, or deny it at our own peril.

How does this relate to His knowledge of the future? He knows what will happen because He's the one who wrote the script. He didn't merely record the events. No. He is intimately involved in the process of creation. He knows what will happen because He's the one who planned it to happen. He's the writer, director, producer.

When we speak of broken plans and dreams that we may have, this doctrine offers incredible assurance. It tells us that God knows every detail of our pain, our hope, our fear. He sees and understands it all. Nothing escapes Him. He not only knows the facts, but the feelings and agonies behind the facts. Like the writer to the Hebrews said, "For since He Himself was tempted in that which He has suffered, He is able to come to the aid of those who are tempted" (Hebrews 2:18). He not only knows us, He knows what it's like to be us, to be inside us. In a sense, His omniscience (and omnipresence) allows Him to be in us and apart from us at the same time.

This provides us with tremendous hope and joy because it means there is one Person in the universe who understands us completely, right through to the heart.

Omnipotence

God is omnipotent. All-powerful. God can do anything that coincides with His nature. That is, for instance, He can't sin. Theologians have argued about this, posing absurd questions like, "If God is all-powerful, can He create a rock which He Himself could not lift?"

They turn omnipotence into a logic game. They take omnipotence to mean He can do illogical things, too. That's not the point.

Omnipotence means God can do anything He chooses to do. He has no limits. He has absolute freedom, no restraints. His omnipotence, like His omniscience, is complete, effortless, instantaneous, and unopposed. No one can overcome Him. It means that He can and will carry out the plans which His omniscience and wisdom make.

Remember Psalm 33:10? "The Lord nullifies the counsel of the nations; He frustrates the plans of the peoples." It's similar to David's words in Psalm 2 where all the nations gather against God and His Son and challenge them to a fight. They want to stage a coup, cast Him off the throne, and put themselves there in His place. What does God do in such a situation? "He who sits in the heavens laughs, the Lord scoffs at them" (Psalm 2:4). Why? They're little Napoleons who have no idea who He is and what He can do. It's worse than a five-year-old challenging Mickey Mantle to a duel, saying he can strike the slugger out. God holds the universe in the palm of His hand. So we think we can fight Him because we can throw a javelin? Not likely.

Omnipotence means God's will and decrees will happen. Nothing He plans can be subverted, diverted, inverted, or controverted. Like He said to Job, "Will you really annul My judgment?" In other words, "Do you have the power to countermand Me?" Never.

God's power is effortless. He doesn't have to try it one way and if it doesn't work, try another. No, when God exercises His power, it's complete, perfect. He can create out of nothing at a word (as He did on the first day of creation) or take something already created and make it into something else (as He did in taking Adam's rib and making Eve).

It's something that should give us great joy. This God who is that powerful is on our side. He's for us. He loves us. Why would anyone dare to oppose Him?

Omnipresence

Third, *He is omnipresent.* Everywhere present.

Again, sovereignty demands that God be "everywhere present." David spoke of this also in Psalm 139. "Where can I go from Thy Spirit? Or where can I flee from Thy presence? If I ascend to heaven, Thou art there; if I make my bed in Sheol, behold, Thou art there. If I take the wings of the dawn, if I dwell in the remotest part of the sea, even there Thy hand will lead me, and Thy right hand will lay hold of me" (Psalm 139:7-10).

But omnipresence means that God is everywhere present *in His entire person.*

We have a sense of this when we pray. His Spirit within us assures us that God hears our prayers and gives us His personal, undivided attention. But how could this be if He is not omnipresent? If it wasn't, we'd have to line up and make appointments to pray on a worldwide scale. And certainly God would collapse from the overload.

But He *is* omnipresent. He occupies every place in space and out of space, in time and out of time in the fullness of His person. It's not that a part of Him is here or there. But He is present with His complete being everywhere. He doesn't parcel Himself up. He has the power to be everywhere at once without diminishing Himself.

This is something totally alien to us. No human can be two places at once, let alone *all* places at once in the past, present, and future. With man it is impossible, but not with God.

God's omnipresence is one of the most comforting elements of His character when it comes to our shattered dreams, for it means that wherever we are, in the pits or on Cloud 9, He is—in His faithfulness—there with us. Nothing less than complete attention and understanding comes our way. We have a God who is intimate and personal to everyone who calls themself His.

Like the Lord Jesus Christ said to His disciples just before He ascended, "I am with you always, even to the end of the age" (Matthew 28:20). Wherever we are, He is. We cannot hide from Him or lose Him in the crowd. We can perch ourselves on a mountaintop, or take a submarine to the depths of the ocean, and He is still there. Remember when the first Russian cosmonaut went into space? One of the first things he said was, "I don't see God." But God was there, completely and fully.

Self-Existent, Self-Sufficient, and Eternal

He is self-existent. When God told Moses His name was Yahweh, or "I am who I am" (Exodus 3:14), He was making an incredible statement about the nature of His being. In essence, it tells us three elements of God's nature. First, His self-existence. That is, He had no cause. He had no origin. He has no one in power over Him. He answers to no one. He is Himself the beginning and end of everything. That's why He said, "I am the Alpha and Omega, the beginning and the end" (Revelation 22:13). Isaiah 43:10,11,13 declares, "Ye are My witnesses ... and My servant whom I have chosen, in order that you may know and believe me ... before Me there was no God formed, and there will be none after Me. I, even I, am the Lord .... Even from eternity I am He."

He is self-sufficient. He has no needs. This means He doesn't even need us, our worship, our praise, our acclaim, our friendship. He is entirely complete in Himself. There is nothing He has needed, can need, or will need. The entire universe depends on Him, but He depends on no one (Isaiah 43:7, 44:24, 45:18).

He is eternal. Before creation was, He was. After it's gone, He will be. He doesn't grow, change, learn, or unlearn. He doesn't become better or worse. As the book of Revelation puts it, He is the God who "is, who was, and who is to come" (Revelation 1:8, 4:8). He has always existed and always will, and He is the only One who is like this. Everything else came from Him.

These truths about God offer us tremendous hope when it seems as if our plans are not God's. They mean God can never be bribed to do wrong, forced to go against His will, or be so overwhelmed by personal need that He would take actions He might regret (like the person who steals money because he sees no other way to pay his bills).

Moreover, it means God based His plan on Himself alone— His perfection, His wisdom, His knowledge, His goodness— not the changing whims of people.

That gives us all hope because it assures us we have an all-competent Creator at the helm, not a man who suffers from indecision. That's one thing people admire most in a leader. "He's a man who stands on his principles. He's a leader who does right even if everyone else does wrong."

There are few such leaders, but above them all stands the great "I am." God rules. He made His plans before the first second of time ticked off. He knows where we are headed, and He'll get us there. Absolutely.

What do these truths say to us when our best-laid plans go awry? They assure us that even though our plans have failed, God's haven't. His plan is the best one. Therefore, we can rejoice that our less than perfect plans didn't happen.

He is holy. If we were to hold a poll and ask what people

thought was God's greatest characteristic, people would reply in many ways. Social activists might say, "His justice." The emotional might reply, "His love." The great sinners might suggest, "His grace." A scientist might answer, "His omniscience." But any true theologian would have to reply, "His holiness."

The primary attribute the seraphim magnify with their august, worshipful praise is, "Holy, holy, holy" (Revelation 4:8).

But what is holiness? We tend to think of it as God's morality, His unwillingness to sin or commit evil. That's part of it.

But above all, holiness means separateness: God's utter distinction from us, creation, and everything else. That God is holy means He remains light years from us in any comparison of qualities, characteristics, or personal abilities. When 100 meter contestants line up to race, the time difference between first place and eighth place might be two-tenths of a second. When Nixon and Kennedy battled for the votes of Americans in 1960, Kennedy won by an average of a half-vote per precinct. When we buy a Macintosh computer over an IBM, the dollar difference might be less than pocket change. But when you compare God to anything else, the gap is infinite. They're not only not in the same league, with God there is no league. He possesses a uniqueness that puts a period on the end of unique. No one else is like Him. No one is even close. Take away your yardsticks, your micrometers, and your light years. God's completely off any scale we might understand.

Holiness calls for one response: awe. All we can do is stand back, bow our heads, and say, "You are worthy of everything. No request is too great. No command is too difficult. I owe You my life."

Holiness means:

God is infinitely majestic; therefore, we owe Him our worship.

God is infinitely moral and righteous; therefore, we owe Him our loyalty.

God is infinitely opposed to evil; therefore, we owe Him our repentance.

God is infinitely serious about His glory being His alone; therefore, we owe Him our awe.

As the author of Hebrews said, "It is a terrifying thing to fall into the hands of the living God" (Hebrews 10:31). That terror proceeds from His holiness, His complete and utter personhood demanding respect, absolute adoration and reverence.

For the Christian who wails and complains because his personal plans have failed, it suggests we've forgotten who God is. We are not our own (I Corinthians 6:19-20). Our plans aren't paramount. We're not what life is all about. Rather, it's God we are here for. He should be the focus of our plans and hopes. His holiness reminds us to stop looking at ourselves and to look up—with reverence, awe, and gratitude.

We tend to think things should go our way; we deserve such and such, and have a right to thus and so. But that's not true. It's a line we've willingly swallowed, but the hook on it is selfishness and pride. It is the holiness of God that reminds us, "This is my program, not yours."

Transferable Qualities

Still, we've only looked at God's unique attributes, things which are true only of Him, and which none of us can ever achieve. On the other hand, there are those qualities which He can share with us.

God is wise. Connected to His omniscience is perfect wisdom. God doesn't simply know the facts, He understands how to use them perfectly for the highest benefit and glory. He employs His knowledge to accomplish the best ends, not just *an* end. As Romans 11:33-36 says, God's wisdom is perfect. He knows precisely what to do in any circumstance. No problem is too great for Him. No question throws Him into a tailspin. No circumstance defies His ability to cope. His wisdom is, in fact, as instantaneous as His omniscience. He knows the facts and how to use them immediately. He doesn't have to learn through trial and error or anything like that.

The astonishing thing is that that wisdom is ours for the asking. James 1:5-6 assure us, "But if any of you lacks wisdom, let him ask of God, who gives to all men generously and without reproach, and it will be given to him. But let him ask in faith without any doubting . . . . " Even if we can't see His wisdom at a specific point in our lives, once we get the whole picture in eternity, we will realize He did all things perfectly.

Again, as we weigh this quality against our struggle with our own shattered plans, we can realize a remarkable truth: God in His wisdom planned at times that our plans would fail. He knew precisely what we wanted and He did not cause those hopes to come to pass because He, in His absolute wisdom, saw that it would not benefit us or His ultimate glory.

I sometimes think of God's wisdom in reference to something I once saw on the beach. A toddler was eating a bit of chocolate, and it got all over everything. What was worse, he still had quite a chunk left in his hand, and it was covered with sand. Mom finally noticed and went into action. She took the chocolate away and cleaned the lad up—all in the midst of loud wails, tears, and screams. Liken that to one of our august plans—a chunk of sand-covered chocolate in our palm.

But God takes that delectable morsel away, and we're frustrated, angered, upset. We may even pout, scream, and cry.

A few minutes later, I watched that mom go up on the boardwalk with her little one and return. But this time that boy walked along as the proud owner of a six inch lollipop.

Liken that lollipop to God's plan. He, in His wisdom, takes the sand-covered chocolate out of our hands and gives us something far better. The problem for us is the delay between loss and gain. But because He is wise, He knows how to deal with that, too.

When we grasp the truth of God's wisdom, that He made His plan out of the bedrock of eternal, flawless, infinite wisdom, then we can trust Him about the things that go wrong. And all the things we do not understand.

God is just. Another transferable quality. We applaud justice; we cry out against injustice. But God, more than any of us, is perfectly just. In the context of His overall plan, we might not see it. The Mafia godfather gets off. The drug dealer receives parole after only a year in prison. The Wall Street billion dollar master heister plea bargains his way into a reduced sentence. The wife abuser never even comes to trial; his wife won't press charges. The abortionist finds himself applauded in a decadent society.

These things outrage us. "Where is God's justice?"

Many times it's postponed. As someone said, "God doesn't settle all His accounts in one day."

Many times other factors overrule, too. His grace. His mercy. His forgiveness. Even though He never compromises His justice (for in the end we'll see that He was both just and merciful), He sometimes appears to do that. That's because He's working with something utterly unique—evil.

Look at Adam and Eve's sin in the Garden. God didn't kill them outright and start over. God's justice waited until Calvary. There, God worked out His perfect justice for all who sin and repent.

But what about those who never believe? God's final judgment will come at the Great White Throne (Revelation 20). In the end, perfect justice will have been served. Psalm

89:14 declares, "Righteousness and justice are the foundation of Thy throne; lovingkindness and truth go before Thee."

God is love. Agape. Unconditional love. Perfect, uncompromising kindness, goodness, faithfulness, and mercy. Everything God does is filled and wrapped with love. "God is love," was the Apostle's testimony in I John 4:16. That doesn't mean God is a romantic, feeling like we do when we look at someone we care about. Rather, God's very being is infused, directed, counseled, and fed by love. Even sentencing sinful people to eternal hell will be an act of love, much as we can't understand that, just as His discipline is wrapped with love.

Again, we can find tremendous encouragement in such truth. It means that God's eternal plan and every element of it felt the touch and fire of love. We might not see it. How is cancer love? How is AIDS love? How is a baby left in a dumpster love?

We can't focus on some specific evil and say it's love or an act of love. What we must do is take to heart God's words in Romans 8:28: "And we know that God causes all things to work together for good, to those who love God, to those who are called according to His purpose." For anyone committed to the Lord and His kingdom, God will take those things and work them for good—that we might be conformed to the image of Jesus Christ.

That's why, when we see some grand plan of ours crash, we must remember that God is love. It was love that allowed that plan to die. And love that will bring the greatest good out of its demise.

God is gracious. Grace. Unmerited favor. That's the theological definition. God has a giving heart. He gives far more than anyone could ever give back. He gives and keeps on giving unaffected by moods or feelings. It's the fundamental truth of grace. "God gave His only begotten

Son, . . . " "God demonstrated His own love toward us, in that while we were yet sinners, Christ died for us, . . . " "We love because He first loved us."

One of my favorite texts is Ephesians 2:4-7. "But God, being rich in mercy, because of His great love with which He loved us, . . . made us alive together with Christ . . . in order that . . . In the ages to come He might show the surpassing riches of His grace in kindness toward us in Christ Jesus." The "surpassing riches of His grace." What's that? Everything God is, God has, and God can do. What will He do with it? Pour it out on us. Astonishing! And why? Because we deserve it? No. Because He has this compulsion to give? No. Then why? Because He wants to. It's His nature to be gracious, to give even when He knows our ingratitude.

Three Thoughts

God's wisdom. Ours for the asking. God's justice. A foundational part of His nature we should remember. God's love. Freely given. Ours to accept. God's grace. Exemplified in His gift of salvation through His only Son. Ours to receive.

What will you do with these truths? Simply stow them away in your mental attic to pull out on a rainy day? I hope not. Three things should stand out.

First, God knows what He's doing.

An incredible statement, isn't it? That's like saying Babe Ruth was able to swing a bat. Or Albert Einstein was decent at arithmetic. Or Abraham Lincoln spoke up now and then.

"God knows what He's doing!"

Have you ever accused Him of not knowing—of messing up your life, of leading you down the primrose path and dumping you in a ditch? I'm ashamed to admit it, but I have. Usually when *my* grandiose plans aren't working out.

Thank God He knows better. In fact, He not only knows

what's best, but what's perfect. What will ultimately yield the highest benefit in life. What will give each of us, not just a taste, but, a full course of glory.

Second, God can be trusted—completely—to turn everything out right.

Like Solomon said, "Trust in the Lord with all your heart, and do not lean on your own understanding. In all your ways acknowledge Him, and He will make your paths straight" (Proverbs 3:5-6).

Notice that. "Trust in the Lord." "Do not lean on your own understanding." What does that mean? Simply this: Quit looking at things as they appear; learn from the Lord. Quit trying to figure everything out for yourself; let yourself relax in God's hands. Quit worrying; start trusting.

Third, live that trust.

Remember when Jesus said that unless we believe like little children, we'll never enter the kingdom of heaven (Luke 18:16-17)? Why did He say it that way? Because healthy kids in healthy families usually just trust their moms and dads. They don't question, interrogate, cast aspersions, throw out doubts; for the most part, they simply relax in the knowledge that they don't have to understand if Dad does.

Remember taking trips with your family when you were a kid? Oh, those long drives! But I rarely worried about getting where Dad and Mom were taking us. I never sat in the back seat chewing my fingernails and quaking. I never fired barbs at my dad like, "You'll never get us there." Or, "You really don't know where you're going, do you?" Or, "How come we never plan anything in advance?" I never questioned his wisdom or knowledge (except the time we ended up in Podunk when we were supposed to be in Philadelphia).

No, I just sat back and enjoyed the ride.

That's a kid. We simply assume grown-ups know where they're going, and we trust them.

Who is God but the most competent, wise, and loving "Grown-up" there is? His car is Planet Earth, and He's driving it to its destination. We'll get where He's taking us, whether we chew off our nails or not. So why not enjoy the ride?

Grace

My father has been a living illustration of this quality to me all my life. One day he said to me as I was working in our office, "Have you thought about getting a house yet?" I told him I hadn't. We just didn't have the resources. He said, "Well, you ought to start thinking about it. Your Mom and I will soon be in a position to help you."

I swallowed and went back to my computer.

Months later, my wife and I moved into a new house, due mainly to the fact that my father wanted to help us. I was awed by his largess, kindness, and generosity.

And yet, behind it all, I see God Himself. Sure, it was my father who made the money, wrote the checks, helped with the finances. But I have to look beyond all that to God's plan, the one He planned from all eternity. That act of kindness was included in it. God didn't have to do that. But He did anyway. That's grace.

What Will You Do With This God?

So what will you do with this Lord of heaven and earth? Rail at Him because He didn't fulfill that crazy idea you've been working on? Tell Him you're not going to believe anymore because He hasn't proved Himself worthy? Scream about your melted popsicle?

Or assert your continued confidence and trust in His wisdom?

You choose.

15/THE WRITER BEHIND THE SCRIPT

What makes God do what He has done?

When a prosecutor argues a case in court, he deals with an important subject: motives. What caused the killer to kill, the forger to forge, the thief to thieve? If he can show why, he can win. Motives are critical. We want to know what makes people tick, why they do what they do. We're fascinated by undercurrents, the scenes behind the scenes.

The remarkable thing is that God has told us why He does what He does. The God of eternity has let us into the inner recesses of His heart. Through His Word, He exposes the rawest nerves of His being.

In this chapter, we'll explore the purposes that guide God's eternal plan. They're important in considering our plans. Why? To arouse greater confidence and trust in God.

A Purpose

What is a purpose?

Webster's Dictionary defines it as "an object or result aimed at." A goal. An end. The finish line.

Theologically, we speak of God's "eternal purpose." That's His reason behind His plan. His plan is what happens. His purpose is why it happens. His plan includes multitudes of situations, places, people, and things. His purpose determines how He works in the midst of them.

God's Purpose

What, then, is God's purpose? Where is He taking us?

We can narrow it down to a single statement: His glory. "For the earth will be filled with the knowledge of the glory of the Lord, as the waters cover the sea" (Habakkuk 2:14). "Holy, Holy, Holy, is the Lord of hosts, the whole earth is full of His glory" (Isaiah 6:3). "Indeed, as I live, all the earth will be filled with the glory of the Lord" (Numbers 14:21).

What is God's glory? The Hebrew word carries a number of meanings, including weight, honor, riches, dignity, splendor. A person's glory, though, is those elements of his being that distinguish him as worthy of note and honor. Think of it under several headings:

Net Worth. Howard Hughes possessed a certain amount of glory. So does Ross Perot, the Rockefellers, Hunts, and Kennedys. Because of their vast wealth, people accord them respect when they walk into a room. Because of their financial holdings and dealings, people come to them for advice, help, a handout. When they speak, people listen.

Apply this to God. Part of His glory is the fact of His vast wealth—the whole universe.

Frankly, I can't imagine the extent of God's wealth. It's infinite. Ft. Knox is a penny bank compared to His. I know how I've felt when I've walked into a rich man's house. But how do I feel in God's? The response God desires when we see His glory is reverence, respect, worship.

Net Power. Just answer the phone and hear the words, "This is the President of the United States," and you'll probably suck your breath in right down to your toes. When you finally quiver a reply, it would probably be, "Yes, *Sir*!" The person to whom they play "Hail to the Chief" is no little Indian. He possesses authority, and with that authority comes a certain grandeur, an aura, a glory.

What about God's power? Have you ever watched a real lightning storm? Or tried to create a rose—a real one? Or a kangaroo? Or an Albert Einstein?. That's God's kind of power statement. How about the parting of the Red Sea? Or that last Battle of Armageddon?

To say God is powerful is a little like saying a nuclear explosion makes some noise. Or the Discovery space shuttle moves. God's power is on such a grand scale, we can't compete or even comprehend. All we can do is slacken our jaws in wonder.

Net Beauty and Perfection. The Scriptures tell us that God is light (I John 1:5). Without light, all things become meaningless, useless. Creation turns into a tactile mystery, hung upside down in gloom. But light exposes the beauties of life. Sparks spatter from diamonds. Blue sky tells us all is well. The rose shrieks, "Look at me!" They are all reflectors of the glory of He who made them.

No one has seen God, but one day we will. We will behold His face (Revelation 22:4). He who created beauty will be beautiful beyond expression. What will we see? Unapproachable, eternal light, so pure, so resplendent, we will fall on our own faces enfolded in joy, transported in worship. I can't imagine it. No one can. It's no wonder God commanded that we fashion no graven image to represent Him (Exodus 20:3,4). Nothing we could imagine could touch His majesty. It would be like picking up a clump of dirt, cuddling it in your arms, and saying, "I prefer this to having a real child."

God reveals part of His glory through His visible perfection and beauty. That's why He created so much variety and beauty in the universe—to offer us a small token of what the real thing will be like for all eternity.

Net Character. Even more than money, power, or abilities, character glows. It's who you are, not just what you are.

Albert Schweitzer. Plenty of people think highly of him. Winston Churchill. Abe Lincoln. Clara Barton.

God puts them all to quaking, grovelling shame. He's love supreme. Grace personified. Mercy without measure. Truth minus taint. Add to that the other things: omniscience, omnipotence, omnipresence, infinite holiness, eternity, Trinity. It's so vast, we can't even comprehend it. Or Him. His character, perhaps, is the one side of Himself that He has revealed more of in Scripture than anything else. Someone has said, "Character is what you are in the dark." It's who you are when no one's looking. Our Lord's character is perfect, through thousands of years of human history, and before that, throughout all eternity.

Can you imagine being patient with an obstreperous four-year-old for a few days? God has been patient with obstreperous forty-year-olds for thousands of years.

Would any of us ever think of giving a gift to someone who loathed us? Yet, God has given—His Son's life in exchange for ours—and continues to give to billions who reject Him.

What greater sacrifice could a man make than to die in place of his friend? None. Yet, for even those who have, in a moment it's over. They're gone. The pain is done. But our Lord paid a price on the cross equivalent to the accumulated pain of an eternity in hell for every person who ever existed. And He did it all, not for us as His friends, but while we were all His implacable enemies.

I don't know how to say it, or think it. God's character is beyond me, or any of us.

I wish I could fashion the words that would somehow capture God Almighty on paper. Or the photographs. Or the painting. Or the music. But nothing can. Nothing will. It will take us all eternity just to begin to fathom the character of this One who has made Himself our personal friend, lover, and Lord.

Net Grandeur. Beauty is personal, something we attach directly to a person's appearance. Power is something you exert. Riches are things you possess. And character is what you are.

But grandeur?

That is something more. It's the complete picture.
Who is God? What word focuses the lens? Majesty?
Magnificence? Exeeding abundance?

Frankly, we don't have a word, except perhaps *glory.* God is
glorious. His glory is forever. It will never diminish, never
fade, never relax, never tarnish. We will behold His glory
forever, and we will worship Him with abandon.

Oh, don't imagine that *that* worship will be anything like the
desiccated variety you find in most churches on Sunday
morning. When we see His glory, every one of us will be
unleashed as master wordsmiths of praise.

The primary purpose of God's plan is that He be glorified.
He desires that we know who He is, from Alpha to Omega. God
has revealed something of His nature and person in creation.
More pieces of the puzzle came together through His
revelation in the Scriptures. Then Jesus walked among us. He
is "the fulness of deity" (Colossians 2:9). He is "the radiance
of His glory and the exact representation of His nature"
(Hebrews 1:3). "Grace and truth were realized" through Jesus
Christ (John 1:17). He "explained" God (John 1:18). The one
who "has seen" Christ "has seen the Father" (John 14:9). Jesus
was the culmination of the revelation process. And the Holy
Spirit bears witness with our spirits that this is truth (Romans
8:16, Hebrews 10:15-16).

Still, there are more elements of the revelation of God's
glory. In the millennium He will reign among us. And in
eternity, we will see His face (Revelation 22:4). God's primary
purpose is that we know Him, in depth, in detail, in heart.

He desires intimate fellowship with you and with me. To
accomplish this, both parties must make an unconditional
and voluntary revelation of themselves. They come honestly
before one another, nothing hidden, nothing held back.
When a creature meets his Creator in that way, what must
happen? The creature cannot hold back: he worships. He

loves. He exalts his Creator. Why? Because he worships voluntarily from the heart.

Think what will happen to you in the very presence of Jesus Christ.

The only word is worship. Unabashed, joy-fired, heart-ringing, soul-elevating, Spirit-exulting worship. We won't be able to restrain ourselves. It will be the natural and spiritual overflow of a heart fueled by love in the presence of his beloved.

And yet, we're talking creature and Creator here. No matter how amazed we might be in the presence of another human who has somehow made a mark on Earth, when we encounter Jesus we will be dealing with greatness and glory on an infinite scale.

God knows that when we see His glory, we'll simply glow in His presence, and worship.

Like Jesus

But that's not His only purpose.

The second element: transforming us into the likeness and character of Jesus. He will make us duplicates of Him—not in looks, not in abilities, not in personal glory—but in character, holiness, and perfection.

All my life I've wished I could become perfect. Sin troubles me. Daily. It binds. It grinds. It tears at the fabric of my soul. I hate it. But one day you, I, and all those who love Jesus will be like Him. It's unimaginable. But it's true.

Think of this as it relates to God's plan. It's not as though God has devised a plan designed to benefit only Himself. No. He has created one for the benefit, exaltation, and eternal joy of all. We are His heirs. He plans to give us *all* His possessions. We are His family. He intends to include us in every family celebration. Never alone in a corner again. Never forgotten or excluded from the guest list. Never saying something that was misunderstood and led to a "falling out." Never speaking out of turn and turning crimson with embarrassment. Never running to your bedroom to weep tears of pain.

That's God's plan. How does it compare with your plans?

Terminate Evil

But that's only the beginning. Another purpose of God's plan is to once and for all terminate evil, every vestige of it. God wants to scour away not only the presence of evil, but the thought of it, the remembrance of it, the seduction of it. Never again will the infection spread. Never again will it crumple a man up in agony. Never again will human murder human. Or lie. Or steal. Or covet. Or think bigoted, hateful thoughts. Or . . .

Remember how it all got started? Lucifer wanted to take God's place (Isaiah 14:14-16). He led a third of the angels in his rebellion against God. "God is not worthy; follow me, I am. God is not good; follow me, I am. God is not loving; follow me, I am."

A third of His creation rejected God, totally, abruptly, brutally, insanely. Then they joined forces and began an all out assault on His kingdom and His people. Their weapons: persuasion through deception (John 8:44). It was desecration through insinuation, annihilation through accusation. God had to cast them out of heaven.

He has chosen to allow sin to run its course, to show in time and space just how evil it is. In effect, God said, "Okay, Satan, you say you have a better way. Fine. Show us. Put it in daylight and demonstrate just how much better it is." In a sense, God was giving Satan complete freedom to "do his thing," the classic "blank check," the right to roam free and wild (Job 1:7). He could go at it any way he wanted.

But God took His own measures to demonstrate His true worth. He set in motion the majestic "plan of the ages," by which He would reveal all there was to reveal about Himself. At the same time, God's war against evil is implacable. His triumph over evil inescapable. He takes Satan's taunts, lies, and deceits most seriously.

In the end, all will agree that Jesus Christ is Lord to the glory of God the Father (Philippians 2:10-11). Yet, not only Lord, but the Great Lord, the worthy Lord, the triumphant, perfect, wise, and enduring Lord. Evil will have its heyday. But it will also get its payday. God will try it finally in His Supreme Court and sentence it to eternal banishment and punishment in hell.

Recently, I had lunch with a salesman for a trucking company, a friend. He told me of a girl in his daughter's "gifted children" third grade class. They staged a mock vote in preparation for the real vote of the 1988 Presidential election. Before the vote, the class was asked if anyone wanted to say anything about why they were voting for whom. A girl raised her hand and stood. She said, "I'm voting for Vice-President Bush because he is against abortion and the other man isn't."

The teacher asked her why she was against abortion. The little girl told the class in a few childlike words that her mother was forty-seven-years-old when she learned she was pregnant. The doctors advised her to have an abortion. They brought tremendous pressure on her, speaking of the statistical chances of having a deformed or handicapped child. Her mother refused to have that abortion. The little third grade girl concluded, "If my mother had had that abortion, I wouldn't be here today."

Yet, to date, since Roe versed Wade and won the Supreme Court's approval of abortion in the United States, some 20 million children have been sacrificed in abortions. Ninety-nine percent of them as a form of birth control.

Evil is running free and fierce in our world.

There are many other examples of the power of sin in our world. For the last two years, my ninety-year-old grandmother has lain in a nursing home, a victim of old age, senility, and a disintegrating body. In Iran and Iraq, proof of chemical warfare has horrified the world. Lebanon lies in shattered ruins after years of conflict. In 1988, Armenia suffered one of the most devastating earthquakes in modern history. The week of the 1989 Super Bowl, Miami, Florida was rocked by race riots. The examples seem endless.

But not forever. There will be an endpoint. God is taking us there. All along, He has been protecting us, helping, guiding, leading, building. One day evil will be confined in hell forever. God will see to it. He's had it all planned from the beginning. And one day His day will come.

The Kingdom

Yet, even this isn't all. There's a fourth purpose in God's plans: creating a kingdom of righteousness that will last forever. With Jesus as its head, us as its co-rulers, we will reign from eternity to eternity.

"And there shall no longer be any curse; and the throne of God and of the Lamb shall be in it, and His bond-servants shall serve Him; and they shall see His face, and His name shall be on their foreheads. And there shall no longer be any night; and they shall not have need of a lamp nor the light of the sun, because the Lord God shall illumine them; and they shall reign forever and ever" (Revelation 22:3-5).

"For behold, I create new heavens and a new earth; and the former things shall not be remembered or come to mind. . . .The wolf and the lamb shall graze together, and the lion shall eat straw like the ox; and dust shall be the serpent's food. They shall do no evil or harm in all My holy mountain" (Isaiah 56:17,25).

"According to His promise we are looking for new heavens

and a new earth, in which righteousness dwells" (II Peter 3:13).

Imagine this new kingdom—God's kingdom. What do you see?

Perfect people.

Celebration.

Fulfillment for all.

Worship.

Thanksgiving.

Jesus—high, lifted up, exalted, and beloved.

I can't grasp it. But one day we will walk with Jesus in person. God intends to inundate us with every good thing He has—forever and ever and ever. I, for one, can hardly wait.

What Do You Say?

What are your dashed hopes and plans next to these? Let me conclude this section with several drawstring thoughts.

First, God formulated His plan with the highest and best motives. His purpose is wholly positive, loving, and gracious. He has considered and provided what is best for all of us. No one is forgotten. We all have our place in His plan.

Second, God's purposes reveal God's heart. Truly, He is "gentle and humble in heart," as Jesus pictured Himself (Matthew 11:29). He laid out His plan in wisdom, built it on grace, fired it through with love, and purified it in holiness. As one of my professors used to say, "His fingerprints are all over it." We can easily say, His "heart-prints have touched every part of it."

Third, God has made it possible for each of us to excel beyond all imagination. You've heard of "being all you can be"? You've considered things like "self-actualization," "personal fulfillment," being a "high achiever," having "lofty ambitions"? Well, this goes beyond all of that. God's intent is glory—for Himself, and ultimately for each of us who are His children.

As Paul said, "For I consider that the sufferings of this present time are not worthy to be compared with the glory that is to be revealed to us" (Romans 8:18).

C.S. Lewis is one of the great Christian writers of all time. Some of my favorites, of all his writings, are his children's series, "The Chronicles of Narnia." If you've never read them, you're missing a major treat. Years ago, when I finished the seventh book, *The Last Battle*, I found myself weeping that I'd never experience that bubbly joy of the "first time through" again even though I've read them several times since.

Yet, it was the last paragraph of *The Last Battle* that has always stuck with me. I reproduce it here as a holy and jubilant reminder of what God's kingdom holds for us in the future:

"And as He spoke He no longer looked to them like a lion; but the things that began to happen after that were so great and beautiful that I cannot write them. And for us this is the end of all the stories, and we can most truly say that they all lived happily ever after. But for them it was only the beginning of the real story. All their life in this world and all their adventures in Narnia had only been the cover and the title page; now at last they were beginning Chapter One of the Great Story, which no one on earth has read; which goes on for ever; in which every chapter is better that the one before" (C.S. Lewis, *The Last Battle.* © London, England, The Bodley Head, Publishers, pp. 183-184).

"The real story." The "Great Story."

That's where we're headed. That's where God's been taking us all along. Can you say with all your heart that that's where you want to go? Is this great adventure part of your plans?

16/The Essential Ingredient

So how do we fit into God's great plans?

Certainly every one of us has had dreams at times in our Christian lives.

A growing, life transforming ministry
The ability to give large sums to the work of God
The desire to lead our relatives, friends, and neighbors to Christ
The ambition to go as far as we can in our work
The desire for a godly, Christ-honoring marriage
The longing that our children will love Jesus and walk with Him all their lives

But what if God's plan doesn't include all those things? What if God's plan has called for you to be a simple factory laborer, just scrimping by all your life? What if His plan requires that you experience acute suffering—blindness or quadraplegia or cancer? What if He planned that you be one of those people who was aborted by a fearful teenage mother who received poor counsel?

These are certainly difficult and unpleasant ideas, yet the "what ifs" can go on *ad infinitum.* What is it that you're experiencing? Higher ambition? Confidence? Greater determination to succeed? Frustration? Anger? Hopelessness?

More importantly, what is the correct response? How do we respond to where God takes us, what He calls us to do or be, what He chooses to make of us? How can we find our peace and satisfaction in Him?

Secret Plan, Moral Will

In a sense, *the first thing the Christian needs to do when thinking about God's sovereign plan for his life is to forget all about it!*

Honest. Concentrate instead on His moral or revealed will.

God's moral will runs parallel with His sovereign plan. It speaks of everything that comes to pass. His moral will relates His commands to us in the midst of that plan.

Does that mean that everthing is set in concrete, and we are all the blind victims of fate?

Not at all. The world uses fate as an impersonal force that works without morality or conviction. It is totally whimsical, doing things without purpose or reason. It is unbiblical.

God is personal, loves us, and works in all of us. His purpose is wholly glorious, perfect, and gracious. But God has chosen to work in a world with people permeated by evil. It's like trying to drive a car with four flats, a broken distributor cap, no gas, and a frozen engine. Worse, it's like trying to direct a car that tells you, "I refuse to do anything you say. Push on the gas, and I'll stall. Throw it into first, and I'll go in reverse. Hit the brakes and I'll speed up."

But God still stands there, repeating the same truths over and over. And God has an eternal plan that determines what He'll do with that car in spite of its rebellion.

A primary truth to realize in living within God's plan is that we make real choices. We have genuine freedom. We can choose to apply His word in a situation, or not to apply it. We can choose to obey a command, or not obey.

When we start worrying about God's sovereign plan for our lives, one of the first things we need to do is forget all about it. No matter how hard we try, we'll never know what that plan is until it's history. We must concentrate, instead, on His moral will as He has revealed it in Scripture. That means knowing the Bible, immersing our minds in it. Treasuring it in our hearts. Meditating on it. As we let God's Word color our thinking and our outlook, we'll face the circumstances of life with God's wisdom. God's power, and God's blessing.

Suppose an architect decides to build a skyscraper. Does he stop and say, "Is this skyscraper really supposed to happen? Does he go to the employers and say, "Give me a sign if you really want me to build this thing"? If they give him the sign, does he turn around and say, "Well, maybe that was too easy. How about another one, just to be sure?"

That's ludicrous. Yet, that's how many Christians approach God's plan. But God has already told us what He wants us to do. His concern is that we apply His truth to our lives.

Faith

If there is a single ingredient necessary to accept the meal of life that God has offered us, it's wrapped in one word: faith. "By faith the men of old gained approval. . . By faith Abel offered to God a better sacrifice than Cain. . . .By faith Enoch was taken up so that he might not see death. . . .Without faith it is impossible to please God. . . .By faith, Noah, in reverence. . . .prepared the ark for the salvation of his household. . . .By faith Abraham obeyed by going out to receive a land. . . .By faith Isaac blessed Jacob and Esau. . . .By faith Jacob. . . By faith Joseph. . .By faith Moses. . . (Hebrews 11). It's faith that enables us to face the twists, turns, tumbles, and topples of life. It's faith that helps us find our way through darkness. It's faith that senses His presence in the valley of the shadow and fears no evil.

But what is faith and how does it relate to God's sovereign plan? Simply put, faith is taking God at His word and acting in accordance with it. Faith has at least five components.

1. Facts. Faith begins with knowledge of the facts. God: who He is, what He is like. Jesus: who He is, what He did, what He's doing now. Salvation: what it is, how you get it. Paul made this clear when he said, "I delivered to you as of first importance what I also received, that Christ died for our sins according to the Scriptures, and that He was buried, and that He was raised the third day according to the Scriptures" (I Corinthians 15:3-4). Before you can exercise faith, you have to have something or someone to exercise it in. Where are those facts? For the Christian, they're contained in the Bible. Learning what it says is the first step on any road to faith.

2. *Agreement.* Faith involves agreement with the facts. You don't just gather information, you agree with it. When Jesus was about to heal two blind men, He asked them, "Do you believe that I am able to do this?" (Matthew 9:28). That called for more than just knowledge of the facts—that Jesus could heal—they also had to believe those facts.

I recall a preacher known for his dynamic speaking delivery. One day at a church banquet he asked a man he didn't recognize if he'd been coming to the church regularly. He had. The pastor then asked if he was a believer. He said, "No, in fact, I don't believe anything you say." The pastor was astounded. He said, "Then why do you come?" "Because," said the man, "I like the way you say it."

Comical, but sad. Yet, there are millions who come to hear the Word preached and their attitude remains that they can take it or leave it. They come to pass judgment on it, as though they could vote on whether it was true or not. But real faith means you agree that the facts of Scripture are the truth, the whole truth, and nothing but the truth. You don't judge them, rate them, degrade them, or add to them.

3. *Internalizing the facts.* Sooner or later there has to be a movement from head to heart. Head knowledge without heart knowledge is empty waste. The facts and your agreement with them affect you in your deepest parts. They move you to action, to change, to conviction. They become rooted in your

heart and soul. They affect and touch every element of your life. You think about them frequently, from morning till night. They spread through your whole being, igniting you with life and conviction. There's an internalization of the truth. Like Job said, "I have treasured the words of His mouth more than my necessary food" (Job 23:12).

4. *Trust*. Faith moves into trust when all these realities—facts, agreement, internalization—are transferred to personal trust in Jesus Christ. If you haven't trusted Jesus personally, the facts mean nothing. Christianity and faith are, above all, personal acts of the heart based on a personal relationship with Jesus Christ as Savior (John 3:16, Romans 10:9-10,13). Like marriage, a bond has been made, a vow, an act of commitment. Marriage involves a legal transaction; faith calls for a spiritual transaction. You move into reliance and dependence on Christ.

When Peter called to Jesus as He walked on the sea, Jesus said, "Come." That was his first act of faith as Peter jumped out of the boat and strode across the water. But when he felt the wind whip his face and the spray lash his cheeks, he let his fear overcome him and he started to sink. That was a lapse in faith. He looked at circumstances, not the Lord. But what was his first cry? The cry of trust: "Lord, save me" (Matthew 14:28-30). When trouble struck, he had no trouble depending solely on Jesus.

5. *Heart transformation*. When all these gears are set in motion, a fifth thing must take place: transformation internally that affects one externally. That involves repentance, obedience, endurance, submission. A person with true faith submits to Jesus as Lord and Master. He follows. He becomes a disciple. He learns. He loves. He worships. He serves. His whole life becomes bound up in Christ. You cannot call Jesus, "Lord," and not obey Him. You cannot accept His salvation without His sovereignty. "Whoever will

call upon the name of the Lord will be saved" (Romans 10:13). No one can truly call on the "Lord" who does not recognize His mastery, kingship, and Lordship over him.

All this relates to God's plan in a simple way. When you have faith and agree with the facts, internalize them, trust Him, and undergo a heart transformation, then you can accept anything as from His *good* hand. Whatever happens, you accept through faith.

Through faith you know that He's in control.

Through faith you're sure He's leading you to heaven.

Through faith you give thanks, even in tough circumstances, because you know He's working it all for good.

Through faith you endure when things go wrong, because you know He's with you.

Through faith you remain confident.

As the writer to the Hebrews said, "Faith is the assurance of things hoped for, the conviction of things not seen" (Hebrews 11:1). It is through faith that you continue to walk even when the ground shakes under you.

Faith Believes The Truth, Even When...

A key truth about faith is that *the man of faith believes the truth regardless of appearances.* He takes what God says as his guide, not what man, the devil, or circumstances imply.

One of my favorite stories in Scripture concerns Elisha and his servant, Gehazi. The king of Aram had decided to liquidate Elisha (II Kings 6). He learned that the prophet was in Dothan, so he gathered all his horses and chariots around the city. Gehazi awakened that morning, looked out, and knew they were in trouble. He ran back in and informed Elisha. "Alas, my master! What shall we do?"

Elisha calmly replied, "Do not fear, for those who are with us are more than those who are with them."

Gehazi glanced around and saw no one on their side.

Elisha noted his servant's fear and prayed, "O Lord, I pray open his eyes that he may see."

God opened them. And what did Gehazi see? "Behold, the mountain was full of horses and chariots of fire all around Elisha."

If anything, faith is a gift God gives us that enables us to see. With our eyes we see light. With our ears we detect sound waves. With our nose, we perceive odors. And with faith we recognize God's hand and care over all our lives.

Faith "comes from hearing, and hearing by the word of Christ" (Romans 10:17). But what makes us able to hear? "It is the spirit that quickeneth. . ." (John 6:63). "For to us God revealed them through the Spirit; for the Spirit searches all things, even the depth of God. . . .Even so the thoughts of God no one knows except the Spirit of God. Now we have received. . .the Spirit who is from God, that we might know the things freely given to us by God" (I Corinthians 6:10-12). "How much more will the blood of Christ, who through the eternal Spirit offered Himself without blemish to God, cleanse your conscience from dead works to serve the living God?" (Hebrews 9:14).

That's why the person of faith believes even when his plans and hopes drown in the surf of trouble. He bears witness to a God of power and love that others cannot recognize unless they also have faith.

Faith Obeys, Even When. . .

Another element of faith is this: *the man of faith obeys even when it looks foolish or against reason.*

Do you want to please God in the midst of trial? "Blessed is a man who perseveres under trial. . ." (James 1:12). Only faith perseveres. Only faith receives a blessing.

Perhaps the greatest example of simple human faith is Abraham when he went up on the mountain to sacrifice Isaac

(Genesis 22). The writer to the Hebrews said that Abraham believed that God was able to raise men "even from the dead" (Hebrews 11:19). Thus, he could obey the command to sacrifice Isaac even though it probably seemed utterly wrong.

How many of God's directives fly in the face of human reason and cunning?

"Love your enemies and pray for them."

"Rejoice always."

"In everything give thanks."

"Do not lay up for yourselves treasure on earth."

"Blessed are the poor in spirit...those who mourn...the meek...those who hunger and thirst for righteousness...the merciful...the pure in heart...the peacemakers."

"Blessed are those who have been persecuted for the sake of righteousness."

"Remember the prisoners, as though in prison with them."

"Let your character be free from the love of money."

All these commands oppose the "wisdom" the world offers. But the man of faith takes them and applies them in life, even though others may laugh, scorn, ridicule, or reject him.

I think of men in Scripture who obeyed God against all normal human wisdom.

Peter and John defying the Sanhedrin about preaching Christ.

David refusing to slay King Saul in the cave.

Noah building an ark when there wasn't even such a thing as rainfall.

Abel offering the best lamb to God.

And Jesus Himself: working with fisherman rather than the sages of the time; giving Himself to a core of twelve men rather than the multitude; taking the insults of fools rather than speak reviling words that might have extinguished their lives immediately; going to the cross, rather than taking His kingdom by force.

To the man of the world these things often make no sense. "Why waste your life?" But to the man of God, it's not a waste; it's the will of God who gave life and who will ultimately reward that life.

Faith Seeks God's Wisdom

Remember another element of faith: the offer of wisdom. How do we cope with the death of our dreams and hopes? By seeking God's wisdom. "If any man lacks wisdom, let him ask of God who gives to all men generously and without reproach, and it will be given to him" (James 1:5). The Greek words here are interesting. "Generously" carries several basic ideas. One is sincerity or simplicity. A second idea means more than enough, all you need and then some. The third thought is "in short" or "in a word." Briefly. His wisdom is simple, brief, easy to comprehend.

"Without reproach" is just as fascinating. It means minus all putdowns, insults, catcalls, and sarcastic remarks.

Ask for wisdom. He'll give it to you. Guaranteed. Not the way you might think, though. He probably won't write it in the sky, or have "a thought occur to you." More than likely, He'll lead you to gain counsel from godly people, study Scripture, or read a biblically-based book on the subject. Wisdom doesn't always come within the hour. Sometimes you have to seek after you ask, and knock while you're seeking.

Remember another thing: God probably won't offer you an explanation for your problem or tragedy. Rather, He'll give you insight into what to do now that your problem has happened. During my seminary years, I went through a dark time and frequently belabored the issue of why. My roommate used to say to me, "You can't ask that question. All you can ask is, 'What do I do now?' God will answer that one."

True wisdom is the ability to cope and overcome your problems, not offer neat psychoanalytical explanations for them. Unquestioning trust in the Creator God is part of the honor we owe Him. Or—trust that may ask the questions but not stop to agonize or demand answers. There is much in life for which we will never know "why."

Faith Knows What True Welfare Is

Consider another thought from Jeremiah 29:11-14. " *'For I know the plans that I have for you,' declares the Lord, 'plans for welfare and not for calamity to give you a future and a hope. Then you will call upon Me and come and pray to Me, and I will listen to you. And you will seek Me and find Me, when you search for Me with all your heart. And I will be found by you,' declares the Lord, 'and I will restore your fortunes and will gather you from all the nations and from all the places where I have driven you,' declares the Lord, 'and I will bring you back to the place from where I sent you into exile.' "*

Many Christians claim these verses as a promise that God will bring "welfare" and not "calamity" into their lives. They interpret welfare in many ways—sometimes to mean the whole "wealth, health, and prosperity" gospel, and other times to mean that you "will fare well," as the word indicates.

Is this a legitimate claim?

Examining the context of Jeremiah 29, we find that this is part of a letter he wrote to the exiles in Babylon, some three thousand of them who had been taken there in 597 B.C., as part of God's punishment on Judah for idolatry. It was meant as a guideline for how to conduct themselves while in Babylon (29:4-7), a rebuke to certain false prophets who pretended to speak for God (29:8-10), an indication of how long they'd be in captivity and what would happen afterward (29:10-14), and a prophecy of doom for the false prophets (29:15-23). This letter, then, should apply only to that select group of people. It was not meant as an all-encompassing statement of God's will for everyone.

Yet, even though this applied specifically to the Jews in Babylon, we can see the same principles at work today (and in other texts) as promised to Christians.

If we apply Jeremiah's prophecy to such ideas as. . .

God wants us to experience His peace that passes understanding

God will listen to us

God desires that we be saved

God will always be available to us

God longs that we rest in Him and not live burdened, broken lives. . .

then we can be sure the principle applies. God does have a plan for us that includes welfare, and not calamity.

On the other hand, if we're thinking in terms of. . .

perfect health

wealth

easy-to-solve problems

no personal harm or persecution

dying in our sleep under warm bed covers. . .

we're thinking non-biblically. God has not promised those things at all.

We need to understand what His plan is and react accordingly. We don't exist for our pleasure, but for His pleasure. The wonderful fact, though, is that when we please Him, we please ourselves. That's the way He made us.

Faith Seeks True Fulfillment

Remember a fifth principle: *true fulfillment comes in pleasing our Lord and Master, not in "doing our thing."* The Me generation has sold us that lie. We tend to think real freedom is discovered only in total independence, through doing exactly as we please and nothing more.

But that's nothing but rank selfishness. It leads down to hell, not up to heaven. Hell will, in a sense, be the ultimate deprivation. The rejector of God receives precisely what he has asked for: nothing of God, nothing from God, nothing for God. That includes food, air, water, earth, friends, conversation, entertainments—everything. Hell will be agony because he'll still have all those desires, but won't be able to satisfy them because he's rejected the One who can give the things that satisfy.

We fit into His plan by knowing His Word and applying it in our lives. Everything else which He hasn't revealed—our mate, our occupation, our ministry—will come together in the context of obedience.

If you're seeking to know God's will here's a simplified version: (1) study His Word; (2) memorize it and meditate on it; (3) obey it in every circumstance of life; (4) seek its wisdom for any specific problem you may have; and then, (5) do what you want to do. If you're living in obedience to what He has revealed, He'll lead you to find out anything He hasn't revealed.

Remember Psalm 37:4? "Delight yourself in the Lord, and He will give you the desires of your heart." What does this verse teach?

"Delight" pictures an abandoned pleasure in Him, an enjoyment of Jesus, a passion for Jesus. Fellowship. Friendship. Doing things together. Including Him in everything. Fascination.

And what if you do this? Then He "will give you the desires of your heart." Does that mean He'll give you anything you want? Right. But first you have to delight in Him. And, as you delight in Him, you're going to be transformed by Him. In other words, your desires will change. In fact, the more you delight in Him, the more your desires will come into line with His plan.

Think of it this way. Suppose I decide that I want a hefty raise from my boss. That's the "desire of my heart." What do I do?

Well, I could stomp into his office, curl my lip, and snarl, "I want a raise. I deserve one and I better get it, or I'm going elsewhere."

How much action would that get?

Not much, if your boss is typical. He might even say, "There's the door, buster."

But suppose I begin to apply this principle to that situation. I delight in my boss. I visit him daily. We have long conversations. I get to know him intimately, his concern for the bottom line, that our company do well, that everyone work together. As he communicates these things to me, I begin to do them. I work at increasing our profits, mitigating our losses. I do everything to promote our company and its image. I lose myself in my work. I seek only to please my boss. I become the perfect team player. Then one day my boss calls me in. I may even have forgotten about my dream of a hefty raise. He sits me down and He says, "Harry, I want you to know I've been watching you." (Isn't that how all bosses start?) "And we've decided to do the following:"

1. Make you a Vice-President.
2. Triple your salary.
3. Send you to Hawaii with your family for a long vacation—six weeks.
4. Provide you with a company car—the top of the line.
5. Give you a 50% bonus each year.
6. And, put your office next to mine so we can talk and be together any time you want.

"How's all that sound?"

You don't even need to answer. You're astounded.

The first situation is the way many of us come at God. The

second is the way He wishes we would.

Now I'm not saying that God plans to give you a raise or a vacation to Hawaii. No, I'm saying that when you delight in the Lord, He will give you far more than you could ever desire. And He will change the desires of your heart so that they are the ones He would give you.

Faith Is Built On Humility

There's a sixth element of fitting into God's plan that is critical: Humility.

"Humble yourselves in the presence of the Lord, and He will exalt you (James 4:10).

"Humble yourselves, therefore, under the mighty hand of God, that He may exalt you at the proper time" (I Peter 5:6).

What is this humility in "the presence of the Lord"? It's a recognition of who He is in relation to who we are. He is the Creator; we are the creature. He is the Father; we are the child. He is the Sovereign; we are the citizen.

Humility involves several things.

1. Submission. The humble person understands that he owes everything to the Lord—his obedience, his love, his endurance. He submits. Like the horse that has been brought under the control of the rider, like the ship that responds to the helmsman's hand, like the soldier who follows his captain's command, the humble person does not see himself as exalted. He is only important insofar as his master is important. God's plan is paramount to him. He desires that God be glorified, that all the world know His greatness.

2. Teachability. The humble person is willing to learn. He seeks understanding, but not in a combative, accusing manner. Rather, he waits on his teacher, expecting that He will show him the truth in His own good time. He's eager for insight and wisdom. He only asks, "What do you want of me?"

3. *Praise.* The humble man praises his Lord because he sees Him as worthy of that praise. He does not exalt himself, thinking the world should be centered about him. He offers sincere, godly praise in response to God's glory.

4. *Thanksgiving.* Only the humble person can "in everything give thanks." He sees it all as the good gift of a good God. He displays a consistent attitude of gratitude.

5. *Self-effacement.* The humble man remains self-effacing, often unaware of the kind of response his presence provokes in others because he's so fixed on ministering to them.

Perhaps the great missionary to China, Hudson Taylor, captures the outlook of the man of humility better than any. Several ladies in Shanghai asked his wife if Mr. Taylor was ever tempted to be proud. She didn't know the answer, so she asked him. Hudson was surprised. "Proud about what?"

"About all the things you've done."

He shook his head and said in wonder. "I never knew I had done anything."

We humble ourselves in the presence of God by accepting whatever comes from His hand with joy and hope. The Apostle Paul frequently spoke of events going against him. But one that always struck me was his problem of the thorn in the flesh. Three times he beseeched God to take it away. But God's plan was different from his. The Lord told Paul, "My grace is sufficient for you, for My power is perfected in weakness" (II Corinthians 12:9).

Paul was not made of arrogant earth. He answered, "Most gladly, therefore, I will rather boast about my weaknesses, that the power of Christ may dwell in me."

What an incredible attitude in the face of trying circumstances. His desires overturned! Yet, still he would press on, confident that God's plan would conquer.

Faith Can Rejoice And Give Thanks

There's a seventh element of fitting into God's plans: Rejoicing. "Rejoice in the Lord always; again I will say, rejoice!" (Philippians 4:4).

Rejoice "in the Lord." That's a highly specific form of rejoicing. It comes only through an awareness of the greatness and presence of God. Only the Christian who has thoroughly absorbed the truths of God's person and character can rejoice when things get rough.

What precisely is it about God that you can rejoice in?

First, because you know God is teaching you endurance. James 1:2-4: "Consider it all joy, my brethren, when you encounter various trials; knowing that the testing of your faith produces endurance. and let endurance have its perfect result, that you may be perfect and complete, lacking in nothing."

Endurance has a high place in God's mind. Endurance, that is, in faith. The most praised church among the seven in Revelation 2 and 3 was the church of Philadelphia. Why were they so praised? Because they "kept the word of My perseverance" (Revelation 3:10). Plenty of people can run 50 yards and score big. A lot can do the 100 or the 220. But it's the marathoners we admire the most. They persevere.

Whenever you face the reality of dashed dreams and halved hopes, remember this: God is much more concerned to make you like Jesus than to make you a winner.

Second, because you know that what's happening to you now is nothing compared to the glory you will see then. I love Paul's words in Romans 8:18: "For I consider that the sufferings of this present time are not worthy to be compared with the glory that is to be revealed to us."

That mentality is difficult to get let alone keep, especially in our world of luxury and comfort. How then do we get it? By setting our minds on the things above. (Colossians 3:2) Fill your mind with His Word. See precisely what it is that He promises. If you can read Revelation 21–22 without longing for heaven, then maybe you're not really thinking about what life is like here. Beverly Hills may feature a few fine mansions. Paris holds some nice art museums. New York has Broadway. But heaven has Jesus Christ—hallowed worship, no pain, no tears, perfect relationships, love, joy, peace, goodness, the music of all the ages. Free yourself from the illusions of this world. Remember Hitler, Stalin, and Idi Amin? There may be more of them just around the decade. I, for one, long that Christ come today, even before I finish this book!

Third, even in ruined plans, we are achieving an overwhelming victory. That victory is character—the attitude, the holiness that comes through trials, not worldly success. Paul pinpointed this truth in Romans 8:37: "But in all these things we overwhelmingly conquer through Him who loved us."

In what do we overwhelmingly conquer? Look at Romans 8:35-36. It's all dashed plans and broken dreams: "Tribulation, distress, persecution, famine, nakedness, peril, sword, being put to death all day long."

What is our victory? That like Christ, we are rising above evil, doing right, and pleasing God. That's the only victory worth fighting for.

Why You Endure

If even now you're looking at broken hopes and crumbled dreams, maybe you're asking yourself the question, "Why does the Lord even let me keep on living? Why doesn't He simply take me home?"

"It is for discipline that you endure; God deals with you as with sons, for what son is there whom his father does not discipline?" (Hebrews 12:7).

That's the final principle of faith in the face of the circumstances God brings into our lives: Discipline. Making us like Christ. Training us. Transforming us. That's the purpose of this life.

All that matters is that you and I are becoming more like Jesus Christ every day. That's God's whole purpose for keeping us alive.

Paul wrote some potent words in Philippians 3. "But whatever things were gain to me, those things I have counted as loss for the sake of Christ. More than that, I count all things to be loss in view of the surpassing value of knowing Christ Jesus my Lord, for whom I have suffered the loss of all things, and count them but rubbish in order that I may gain Christ, and may be found in Him, not having a righteousness of my own derived from the Law, but that which is through faith in Christ, the righteousness which comes from God on the basis of faith, that I may know Him, and the power of His resurrection and the fellowship of His sufferings, being conformed to His death; in order that I may attain to the resurrection from among the dead" (3:7-11).

Meditate on those words. Drink them. Digest them. Let them color you life. Then take a look at your ambitions. Are they too small? What about your dreams? Are they more egotism? Set your sights on Christ, on knowing Him, on serving Him.

That's all that matters.

That's all that will matter when you stand before Him.

17/Gentle Dreamer, Dream On

Perhaps you've read to this point, and wonder: Should I dream big dreams, have high hopes, and seek to accomplish great deeds for God?

Yes.

Consider Ephesians 3:20-21, a favorite of mine. "Now to Him who is able to do exceeding abundantly beyond all that we ask or think...."

Look at that: "Him who can do *exceeding abundantly*..." That's an exciting expression. It means a superabundance! An overflow so far beyond anything that, Paul says, we couldn't even *ask or think* it! If anything, even the biggest dreamers are nothing more than small thinkers when it comes to what our Lord can do. So never say you can't dream big dreams as a Christian. God says we can't dream big *enough* for Him!

At the same time, what we can't do is dream wrong. That leads to disillusionment. That's where too many Christians get off target. Once that happens, they think God must be wrong, not them. They say they'll never trust Jesus again. Not completely. There will always be that reservation, that hesitation, that holding back.

No, God wants us to dream, to seek to achieve, to strive for the sky. But do it on the basis of His word. "Seek first His kingdom, and His righteousness; and all these thing shall be added to you" (Matthew 6:33).

What's the result? "All these things will be added to you." Food—(not necessarily *cordon bleu*), shelter—(not necessarily a mansion), clothing—(not necessarily designer labels). God will meet our basic needs. Anything else is grace. But His promise is that He will provide for our needs, always.

The person who seeks His kingdom and righteousness will never be without a dream. In fact, he'll dream constantly of all the things he wants to do to lodge that kingdom in his community, in his church, in his workplace, in his life. He'll bring the utmost creativity, commitment, and consideration to those efforts. He'll dream bigger dreams than he ever before imagined.

Dreams are the stuff of action, the core of courage, the shield of determination in the face of withering fire. They motivate us to act on the basis of God's Word, and to triumph in the name of His promises.

For the believer, life is more than Shakespeare's tale told by an idiot. Rather, it's a tale recited by God, infused with the life of the Holy Spirit, touched at its core by His love and power. It's often full of sound and fury, but it signifies everything. In the end, we will have seen that tale in all its technicolor, and we will say to Him, "Thou hast done all things well!"

So do you have a dream? Ask yourself, "Is this just my dream—an egotistical, ambitious, self-exalting vision of what I want to do with my life?"

Or is it God's dream—that flawless picture of His kingdom, the inscription of His love on man's hearts, the destruction of all things evil and godless?

How you answer will determine what you do when God doesn't follow your plan.